FACING THINGS

Also by Alistair Elliot from Carcanet

My Country
Turning the Stones

ALISTAIR ELLIOT

FACING THINGS

CARCANET

First published in 1997 by
Carcanet Press Limited
4th Floor, Conavon Court
12–16 Blackfriars Street
Manchester M3 5BQ

A CIP catalogue record for this book
is available from the British Library
ISBN 1 85754 304 1

The publisher acknowledges financial assistance
from the Arts Council of England

Set in Palatino by CentraCet Ltd, Cambridge
Printed and bound in England by SRP Ltd, Exeter

Contents

Acknowledgements and Notes

I am grateful to the editors or literary editors of the following journals, in which most of these poems first appeared: *London Review of Books, London Magazine, Times Literary Supplement, New Statesman*, the *Swansea Review*, the *Spectator, other poetry*, and *Poetry Review*.

One of the poems, 'A Family Wireless', was broadcast in BBC Radio 4's programme *Ode to Hilversum*, produced by Tim Dee. The poem appeared in a shorter form, as a sonnet in fact, in my previous book *Turning the Stones*, and I am grateful to Sean O'Brien for pointing out that I had wrapped it up rather than finished it. I think it is probably finished now.

The poem 'Facing South' is not really related in subject to my near-neighbour Tony Harrison's 'Facing North', but it is the same length and more or less in the same form.

The 'Fairy Flag' is of course the one at Dunvegan Castle, Skye. W. H. Murray devotes a paragraph to it in his *Companion Guide to the West Highlands of Scotland*, but my starting point for the poem was the two very different labels displayed beside it on the wall of the castle drawing room.

'Letter to *Nature*' was sent seriously as a possible contribution (in the tradition of Empedocles and others whose science was published in verse) to the well-known scientific weekly – which returned it equally seriously with a nice rejection slip.

The Euripides chorus referred to in 'Looking Out' is from *Hercules Furens*, and can be found in *The Penguin Book of Greek Verse* (p. 242) in Greek, with a straight-faced translation.

Looking Out

In memory of FB, 1977–1996

All morning we drove north to the Museum
talking, a sort of telephone call
lasting for hours, our eyes ahead
half-focused, with no gesturing at all –
much like conferring with our favourite dead,
the little girls in the back
an immediate taste of other-worldly static.

Aside from what we were saying ran the landscape,
ruined by man; and a grey sky
empty now of the magical alphabet
of travelling birds. For part of my
conscious raison d'être
ici (in North Dakota)
was to see cranes and prairies as they were.

The cranes might have gone forever. I couldn't remember.
What came into my mind like an old tune
between our sentences
was a garbled but indelible line
out of Euripides:
Please, I don't want to live without my mouse –
I mean, without the Muse.

The Muse, I thought, was that electric medium
through whom we clean ourselves and coat the world
in happy theory, the bright neighbour
who finds sweet water in our home field,
who brings plums again to the dried arbour,
the mouse who simply appearing
makes the old cat's eyes shine and its mouth water.

In the Museum there were lots of mice:
soft toys in their own skin, in their own dens
under the roots and other creatures' paths;
and there were cranes, in their glass coffins,
standing in clumps of grass,

no longer prairie and no longer whoopers –
'The species is extinct in Manitoba.'

We saw the tress of blue-stem an inquisitive
man with an idle morning dug to the root.
Deeper than any mouse has ever sounded,
deeper than four men's graves, it sought
safety from heavenly fire, and found it:
the ill-cut hoydenish hair
burnt, or scalped by a scythe, grew back each year.

There was something I still regret we didn't see
in the basement; someone fell on the slippery floor,
but I can't remember who;
another line of that Euripides chorus
returned: *The good should be given two*
runs round the mortal track:
so we had two helpings of ice-cream, then drove back.

Crossing the border was strange: one way so easy,
like overtaking the northbound hem of spring.
Going south, though – were they trying to stop some mother,
like the goddess of breakfast food, from smuggling
out of a world of darkness her small daughter
into the light of American day
for another summer of music, writing and playing?

For something hung over us – the sun's extinction,
stifled by cloud? those anxious drops of rain?
No, the small Frankish girl who was born in Cairo
by the will of Allah had good reason to mourn:
she told me she would lose her friend tomorrow –
Small Bear go camp. 'But I've got her
for eight days in August.' Such is our hold on the future –

Eight days, eight years, or eight decades, a handful
of air accumulating in the palm,
grasped from the window of a moving car,
is all we have, a stretch of time we cram
into our hungry mouths as if it were
something solid:
as if enough of it could be good food . . .

After a day of looking in parallel
at things from your confessional on wheels,
arriving home is hard. We separate,
no longer knowing where to look. The girls
re-enter their absorbing singular fates.
I sink to my cellar room
deep and safe as the grass in that Museum.

Anabiosis

for Don and Jane

Water bears are my consolation
at the moment. The thought of seeing one
is like having a magic booktoken,

the loan of a three-masted schooner,
a free pass to every theatre.
And yet I never heard of them till this year.

They are common, but very small – all but invisible.
In fact, my pen's thinnest calligraphic wiggle
is wider than this animal.

Some day, when I am feeling worse
than now, I shall cash in these creatures,
at present stored in a tiny piece of moss.

Though it's already cactus-dry,
I know they will not die on me.
Some lasted more than a century

in a museum drawer, so why not mine?
All they need is a breath, the word of rain,
to come to life and play again.

Poplars

triste lignum – Horace

The trees appeared to be busy
surrendering, all their arms
held up: Kamerad!,
from a line of Indian gods.

It was a trick, for one
stepped out and clubbed the road
(a few yards too soon)
with a ton of its own wood.

No one came out. It seemed
the silent end of the world
as the summer dust steamed
and the graveyard wall folded.

I knew it was my fault.
No one came out because
this was between my guilt
and the green infernal trees.

That must be why I felt
in the wrong as I left the scene
of punishment unhurt –
as if I had hit and run.

Fatal Mister

Fatale mistero, fatal mister
fatale, fatale, fatal mister
    Verdi, *Aida* (libretto by Antonio Ghislanzoni

I: *Something is after us*

Birds are above us, usually. They sit high
and talk about us. Other animals
take their rough comments as alarm calls,
and you can always feel some careful eye
brushing your skin. The rings of information
around us spread, and reach our enemies.
Then we stand still, to recreate the peace
before we came. The great machine of attention
looks somewhere else – until the beasts that own
the ground we stand on catch our smell and wake,
or maybe angry insects move us on.

Something is always going to attack . . .
But we shall understand it. We are known,
but we can watch it, gnaw it, know it back.

II: *It seems to know everything*

When I went hunting with my father, he
read me the signals, and my mother knew
where I had lost my things and what I do
in the secret place, where nobody can see.

So I saw everything can be understood
by someone older. His cunning made him king,
her cunning overlaid the rules of being
with rules that make us happy if we're good.

I realise now they guessed and didn't know;
I couldn't see they sometimes hesitated.
But when they died and left me here below

I still looked up to them. They had created
a tree of thought, with nests where I could grow
like the wild birds that they domesticated.

III: *We have been given rules, but different rules . . .*

The rules of safety got me here. Your rules
seem dangerous. What you eat is dirty, too,
but you look good. You let my hand reach through
the fence of space into your richer smells.

Does this excitement come from touching you
or breaking rules, and finding they were made
by people, not by something overhead –
faces in leaves, that keep the world in view?

Can we be living for a moment free
from rules? Certainly things I thought I knew
have lost their names. I don't know what I see.

I look with wonder at the world of dew.
I've even found forgotten parts of me,
and all the country that I know is new.

IV: *The rules don't cover everything, but*
    there must be some general answer

I think I understand the world, for here
it is and here I am, and what I do
moves it or hurts me: everything should be clear,
all change being caused by me, or Them; or you.

But air, the invisible thing we travel through,
moves by itself. The sun and stars appear
to move as well; the moon is eaten, too,
and then grows back – like 'summer' every 'year'.

Things fall – they always fall, without a cause.
Is there a cause I cannot understand?

I can't believe things have a common Will –
the Things must be obeying Someone's laws.

Some Mind has made all this, if not some Hand,
and probably lies watching somewhere still.

15

V: *Our answers may get better, but the first were wild*

These explanations are a kind of lie:
I made them up. They cover what I know,
but they are guess-work, date-and-raisin pie –
a little fruit, a universe of dough.

So it surprises me how they acquire
a sort of polish, some solidity
from repetition, and instead of 'liar'
I'm called a 'prophet' by my family.

We easily forget the obvious:
that all we know, or think we know, was seen
or else invented by a human brain –
for something in us longs to hear again
from the inhuman dead, some Angelus
who brings an answer we need not discuss.

VI: *Unfortunately, the early answers have authority*

The possibly becomes a probably;
doubt is outvoted; reason, weeping, yields;
and the great plough of man's theology
divides the unmarked cosmos into fields.
Meaning spreads out along the lines of space
like willowherb in ruins; everywhere
the unexplained acquires a human face:
the lust to understand puts Deity there.

The angel, fatal Mr Mystery,
leads us to battle then – we have to kill
the soldiers of another history,
and die because two guesses disagree.

How does a guess become a certainty?
What turns a fancy into Law, and Will?

VII: *Our minds*

Our minds are dangerous. Or rather, based
at a single point (of course), the private mind

seems in command: the universe marches past
perhaps saluting, certainly inclined.
It's bowing to its laws, though – not to us:
we like it, so we think it's personal –
the self-dug trap of human consciousness:
'There must be Something – The Invisible! –
watching us, as our parents watched us once.'

What did the cosmos watch before we came?
What could it criticise?
                                  The stage was bare,
bare as the whistling auditorium.
Can we imagine rocks learning to care
or oceans losing their indifference?

VIII: *The world*

The whole ball thrills us. In its curve we see
the ancient fullness of our milk-horizon
freed from a cloudy dress. We recognise in
everything an emotional simile.
Nice day, bad sea, strong wind – the imagery
of our own star distorted to an eye-sun
that follows us with kindness or derision –
proved by our shadows – round the gallery.
The gallery's not for us. It has been here
so many thousand million years before
we dropped in, glanced around, and sniffed the air.
There is no meaning and no purpose there,
simply the structures that result from law.
We face it, naturally, with love and fear.

Anniversary Photograph

The bed is rumpled, a crumpled invitation
to a painter not afraid of seeming old-
fashioned, to study fold-
ed light and shade ('Irregular Corrugation').
We stand behind it, sheep-
ish in our morning-wrinkled skin,
in short silks that convey a whiff of sin,
and broad-striped trousers that mean crime or sleep.

I have my arm around you thinking of Stubbs'
portraits of blank-faced couples with their race-
horse and its groom, their prize bull and their carriage
with coat of arms outside their subs-
tantial house and its harvest. Here's our place,
our indoor field, the flattened grass of marriage.

What Big Eyes You Have

I was just showing the cat
how to empty the hot
water bottle. He sat

in the window there, a brown
judicious blur, a frown
of thought lost in fur.

Oh, Mungo must not be bored!
I turned the bottle toward
his pointed face, and poured:

he saw the old water fall
like a snake from a shady hole;
I saw his pupils swell.

It recalled our long ago
talk of the shy ego
hiding what the eyes show,

and how we turned to check
each other's: the soft shock
of vision
        gulping
            the dark.

Crossed References

Solving the crossword: 'Insignificant (8)'
it says. The answer's 'Marginal'.
I see an insect squashed, still delicate
but perfectly flat in a nostalgic smudge
near the top corner of an unread page.
Beyond it, a fringed tablecloth with no table
appears on grass, pinned down with things to eat.
To the left, a river laps. We are on the edge
of a secret, and the caught fly contains it all.

Radios

We are electric beings: when I move
My head between the radio and its mother
Far off, I hear the automatic surf
That fringes my endeavour, the slow stutter
Of thoughts falling and bounding, sentences
Marshalled and led off clinking. My head's noise

Almost covers the message from the world.
The static must be mine, not some machine's
Next door. The perfect words or tunes are veiled
Then stifled by the cloud-talk of my brains.

So in my head: when you approach, my love,
Reception worsens till I turn it off.

A Garden of Earthly Delights in High West Jesmond

Cyrus had a palace there and a large paradeisos
full of wild beasts, which he hunted on horseback
whenever he wanted to strip and exercise himself
and his horses –   Xenophon, *Anabasis*, I.ii.7

This neighbour's garden or back yard
is dear to me. She's told me, if it rains
at night, each worm that it contains
slips to the surface in the dark,
glimmering, for carnal knowledge.
Her brick enclosure is a mating college,
worms' paradise (Persian for hunting park).

I'd heard that when a thrush or blackbird
thumps on a lawn the worms stick out their necks
for rain – but no, they rise for sex,
a pleasure which means twice as much
to a hermaphrodite:
the nearest stranger's always Mr Right;
they match all parts in one delicious touch.

I walked there once: I'd come and watered
her thirsty greenery while she was away.
Two little girls across the way
were giggling, with a naughty plan.
They were too young to know
two round rude bottoms squared in a bedroom window
might seem a smile from nature to a man.

Now, 'If you can't believe my word,'
the neighbour says, 'come round. Some night it rains.'
The yard may show the worms it still contains,
but will the girls, now in their teens,
be there? – trowels in fists,
bent over, budding helminthologists,
their bottoms smiling darkly in their jeans?

22

Auks in the Minch

The green and purple bergs of Scotland melt
so slowly the millennia seem equal:
on such a day Columba could have paddled
    here in his coracle.

In such light airs you approach the razorbills
on breaths of silence, till they patter away
or plunge abruptly at the flap of sails –
    as if they couldn't fly.

Perhaps they can't, in summer – out at sea
with fledglings, in these calms, and full of fish;
but we have seen them braver, dazed with joy,
    flying close when the wind's fresh.

The rollers lifting *Mistral* by the heel
backwards as we surged in by Ardnamurchan
slung the plump birds all round us through wet hills
    crusted with foamy lichen.

Air at that speed must feel as firm a fluid
as water: they can skim along the veins
of either, dreaming as they swim or glide
    of perfect hurricanes,

where the whole party's mixing in mid-air,
the fish have wings, and jellyfish balloons
which lift them off in that wild atmosphere
    where the Gulf Stream begins.

The Fairy Flag

I

The fairy flag is in a frame
like a picture white on white,
like a fine
tablecloth or shoulder-wrap
too good to stain
on anybody's theatre-going arm.

If memory serves, there is some
embroidery on it, plain white stitch,
but no sign
of loops for hauling it up –
though it's twice been flown.
The fairy promised to bring help three times

and they say in 1940 the PM
asked the owner to fly it
to save Britain –
a fairy feathering a Messerschmidt's prop
for Paul Nash to paint –
but the MacLeod said: No, there's worse to come.

II

Another label innocently
tells us the flag is silk, and faded
from being red and yellow – someone
has worn it too much in the sun –
and the cross-stitch is Syrian
work of the twelfth or thirteenth century.

This puts a new complexion on the fairy:
not the misty bath-look of a country lady
mysteriously slim, but the pale brown
of a mysteriously plump, veiled woman
of Damascus, in perpetual afternoon
sewing, secluded from the dusty city.

We wonder how her needlework found its way
to this wall. In the coarse hands of some crusader?

Did he come ransoming her Saracen?
Did she give this silk as a safe-passage token
to the horrible Frank? – who'd have a lot to explain
when he got home to his glowing wife in Skye.

My Gaelic Poem

An oystercatcher is in it. Far away
is the mountain called the milking-stool, the pass
of brindled dogs, the knoll of alder trees
and the corner glen. There is the little loch.
The high hill, where my sister walked with me
and we saw the Minch, has become blonde with snow.
The deer have crossed the shingle to the islands.
The heron flies slowly to the waterfall.
Is it the ghost of an old man, the fisher,
or is it an old woman from the sea?
The seagulls cry together, 'Cailleach, cailleach.'

Bentonite

At the Little Missouri River
the warden was eloquent, to slough
our shoes and socks off.
He wanted to show us more than water
on that hot day: the miracle
of bentonite on the middle-aged sole.

This igneous clay collects
as mud in the shallows:
it squudged between toes
like melting chocolates,
like pure dirt, like whatever one called
the fruit of bowels as a child.

But after the first shiver
of disgust, we became aware
of birds trafficking in the air,
we saw the toothmarks of beaver:
something was suddenly clean –
we had lost our dead skin.

Our feet and hands were smooth
and new – these clay crystals
picked off our broken cells
like nothing else on earth –
old apes groomed by the very stuff
we may be made of.

The Pot

The mound will be dug away
Now where they used to get clay
For the brickyard by the road
From Shiraz to Persepolis.

Passers-by would stop
And climb up to buy pots
From the workmen. The low sliced mound
Was an Achaemenian burial-ground.

On a weirdly overcast day
(For once, a Persian grey)
We paused there. Someone bought
A beautiful pot. But I

Disapproved of digging for treasure.
Archaeological pleasure
Was the thing to aim at. The man
Thought I was trying to bargain

And went down from 'Panj' to 'Chahar
Toman' – a Mars bar.
I held the dusty pot
Light in my hand for a moment.

It would have held a drink.
I considered: No provenance;
Fragile; Contraband –
And put it back in his hand.

He looked at me and smashed it.
So it was only bought
Once – by a mourner who paid
With a coin bearing Cyrus' head.

Well, the pot belonged to the dead.
We should not buy – or sell – it.
Best for us all to become
Bricks, atoms of home.

Premonition

Things are turning up today.
First, the tomato knife –
God how we missed it! –
After six months away
In some underworld life
Is back – I hope, for more than a visit.

Then, my best travel trousers,
Immobilised by zip failures,
Have got over their shame –
I searched for them in three houses
A boat, and their manufacturer's –
They appeared on their rail, at home.

And it's still not noon: I fear
The third return –
You, the lost heroine
Of my lost middle year,
Will click the gate, and burn
The front door down as you glide calmly in.

You will take off my old straw hat
With the hole for each half-cocked ear,
You will take off the nose-bag,
The blinkers, the blanket,
And throw me on the floor
For a last warm and mortal shag.

The wife and family
Stand round like solemn trees –
I smell the carpet
And your recovered body –
The approaching sneeze
Fades. I am leaving the planet.

My Great-Uncle Charles Howcutt (1865?–82)

A cousin of 'Immortal Clay', our 'granny
In Australia' who never saw her children again
After she left them 'at the end of a lane'
Heard of the first death from her daughter Annie:
'Dear Mother, Charles fell under the wheels of the dray.
It was in Northampton. He slipped on a wet cobble.
Being nearest, I was called to the hospital.
I could stay several hours. He died next day.'

His head was crushed. I think he couldn't speak.
She tried to comfort him with sweets, which he
Ground in his teeth to dull the agony.
You'd have expected him to be too weak –
He chewed, though. Ever after, a crunched sweet
Seemed to revive the memory past bearing,
And if her girls had pear-drops for a fairing,
She'd say, 'Remember . . . manners. Suck. Don't eat.'

Mother

Somewhere among the roots of England
my mother found her rules.
Some shy Shakespearean aunt
taught her to eat from fairy circles
and how to name a
tracehorse: Forrest or Homer –

coins from the wordhoard of our tribe
buried in the angelic angles
around home: in Long Chase, the Top,
the Forty-Acre, the Pikel.
School spread on this the alphabet
and the best lines of Scott,

and a cousin from Australia
showed a way to peel an orange
(about the time of Gallipoli)
with a knife, in seconds –
a startling modern skill
in a mediaeval girl –

but she never learned to hold reason
so that it would not squirm.
I puzzled for years over one
bewitching apophthegm:
'Always stir the pan
widdershins, against the sun.'

Now in her old age I
question this cooking-etiquette:
Was it a form of magic?
'What ever made you think that?
Don't you know *If the spoon should turn,*
There your scrambled egg will burn?'

The Mortal Map

Let's buy a large-scale map then and survey
your childhood fields, where George
kindest of brothers
in your cold family
walked you along your brook one day
to find its source, the issue of waters.

Show me the cantle where the cowslips grew,
perhaps still grow;
show me the legendary pool
you pushed your brother Fred into,
and where it might be nice to throw
the powder that was you.

Show me a way there by some unowned hedge,
among the fields where George
found with the plough those Roman coins
he gave you, coins that later Fred purloined
and changed to beer at the Black Bull.
And where, to end my day, is the Black Bull?

But walk me first across the imaginary
contours (redrawn from satellites)
into the silence where your father rattles
his crowscarer still, and his father pulls
the handcart with its load of salt –
crystals of sweat, our chips of memory.

A New Drainage System

The house might look
like part of the suburban
ribbon,
but then it stood alone,
an obvious farm, a landmark
beside the track.

My grandfather
never wanted to join
the round of the cess-cart man.
His new bucket would go on
to some other
less fastidious defecator

and might never come back.
Meanwhile he must coil
his ropes of night-soil
into some foul
neighbour's receptacle
from earlier in the circle.

Moreover the dung
would magnify the yield
of someone else's field –
which he held
unnatural and wrong.
In old age it would still sting.

His daughters, though, enjoyed
the varied spectacle
along this road to school
of how the parish wiped its hole:
squares of newsprint cut
from the Northampton gazette

fluttered in some furrows
among the future sheaves –
Did someone use dock-leaves? –
letters of scorned loves,

the pink and white, richer and poorer
dissolving in the day's weather.

After eight decades
of fading intimacies
and sharpening family faces
they remember the village faeces,
the joke of counting turds,
and seeing what people read.

Erdbeeren, Fragole, Fraises

qui legitis flores et humi nascentia fraga
  – Virgil, *Eclogues*, 3

One autumn day in 1932
My mother, shopping alone (I was inside her),
Bought some late strawberries (Scottish). Dad did too,
Elsewhere. So the strap-hanging inner rider
Might have acquired then his taste for earth-
berries: six weeks before his birth.

The anarchic seeds from the great feast they ate
Worked their way down, met in a cul-de-sac
(Her appendix) and began to agitate.
We all kept calm. The surgeon cut a crack
In my ceiling and took out the rotten bit.
I'd have looked up – but can't remember it.

And the next month my life in air began.
Heroic mother – but she couldn't eat
That fruit again. Her child became a man,
And never noticed. Strawberries were his treat,
And still are, still with feelings of a birthday,
Though sugared, in lemon-juice, the Italian way.

Plants

I knew a rose-snob once. She rooted up
The horrible modern bushes and pushed down
Into the willing earth Elizabethans.
Going back towards dog-roses and wild thorns
Seemed natural to her. I say, why stop
Four centuries ago? Why not go on
And cultivate the pioneers? – who live
In the oceans still, with neither root nor leaf,
Globes with barely a twinkle yet of green.

That's not quite right. Those creatures in the sea
Are descended too, in their self-divisive way,
Sisters or something at billions of removes,
From the first cells. Everything that survives
Is equally new and old: individually
We speed like living galaxies away
From the big bang of biology, that cell
Repeating itself until it had the plural
Of I off pat, on Multiplication Day.

Letter to *Nature*

Things always happen more than once in nature:
an event that is permitted will recur.

'The' Big Bang therefore must be one of a number.

The evidence for this would be left-over
bits of an earlier Bang – an 'ancient' star
in 'recent' space; ripples that interfere
with ours and cause 'our' particles to cohere
instead of simply spreading; alien powder
that should have fallen back, caught in our sphere.

The sums will not add up, of course – Elsewhere
would send us unknown quantities of matter.
But can't we tell if ours is older or younger?

Yours sincerely

Harpoceras at Port Mulgrave

The ammonite lived wherever Yorkshire was
in those days (nearer the equator); died
in a tidal smother of Lower Jurassic mud;
and became a shape in shale, called *Harpoceras*.
Strangely, it had a smell: the iridescence
of a jungle caught in the geological squeezer
had seeped into its chambers, where the creature
might have left recent scent, this carbon essence.

The weakness of the rock conveyed a feel
of the animal lost in diagenesis,
molecules softly interchanging places.
But I left it, thinking to find a better fossil,
and came away empty-handed. Now all night
I have an ache of loss like a young lover,
imagining it abandoned again to weather
after two million centuries, hardly looked at.

I lie awake wondering what it is
that fills the dark with thought: the ammonite,
at least its shape, come back again to light
for a few hours, the time between the tides? –
or my rejecting it? The ache is guilt
at saying no – as if I'd meant to claim
what only time and accident should name:
who shall inherit, who shall leave, the world.

The feeling oozes from the earliest moulds
of memory, moments frozen in the rooms
where I first learned to live, my diagrams
of forces I must yield to or control.
Here are the secret juices of my life
collected in imaginary chambers
and now let flow. A child in there remembers
the gods; the strife; the settlement of strife.

A Family Wireless

You switch it on, pour out a cup of tea,
drink it, and finally sounds of outer space
clearing its throat blow from the vizored face;
pause; then the swelling voice of history
refills our kitchen from the BBC.

It's full of static and authority.
I daren't re-tune it: set before the war
on Home, it doesn't know it's Radio Four.
It never knew the Third, or Radio Three.
It was turned off if it tried Comedy.

We stare at the brown gauze: that mouth-like stain
represents years of electronic breath
reading out sentences of war and death,
names we should know, facts that might entertain,
instructive crime and edifying pain.

The angels of the Lord spoke through that gauze
to us. Was it the innocence of youth
to think an angel told the legal truth?
The cat of veracity may have had its claws
retracted, but we knew its powerful paws:

We'd seen the ruins, and the ships on fire;
I met a boy from Belsen, and a man
maltreated by the aesthetes from Japan.
The cat of history, fed but not for hire,
sits on Big Brother at its own desire.

Those messages continue to engage
our trust. Up there above us, on the wall,
the backdrop of our minds, this oracle
still tells the temperature of human rage:
'Keep calm, the blood is flowing well, off-stage.'

Now it's our mother's link to life, her thread
to safety from the labyrinth of the self.
When it stops talking on the mantelshelf,
that silence of significance will spread
even to the newsless circles of our dead.

Snipers

I

Jock was a sniper, in that war
a very dangerous role:
nothing for miles for anyone to shoot at
but you, on your slight knoll,
inside your artificial tree,
behind your patched wall.

– I only once, he wrote me
with that same trigger finger
curled to the pen, fired
a shot in anger –
at an officer glimpsed in the mist
behind their lines, on a charger.

– I had to decide in a second
which of them to kill,
and chose the horse. I saw the man's
astonished face as they fell.
His mind had been somewhere else.
For all I know it was Rommel.

II

Being about ten,
I tried out my new B.B. gun
not on a piece of paper
with circles crayoned on,
but a squirrel, who ran
at the wrong moment across the lawn,
our coarse-grassed Florida lawn.

He hid the blur
of his scrawny body –
the cloudy shadow of fur –
behind an orange tree,
but looked round at me
just as I fired. I feel the scream
after half a century.

III

The line drawn by his bullet
joins the solitary
actor to reality:
the body of his woman
bleeding on the laundry
makes her sniper human.
Now he can take a break
for a sinful cigarette,
the first he's earned this week.

Perhaps he feels no guilt
this minute;
only relief
at something to tell his chief.
It may take years to find
the verdict of his own mind,
a reminiscent smile
or an inner yell
that attempts to recall
the tiny deaf missile –
escaping faster than sound.

An Old Shaving Brush

Soaped up for his last shave
presumably by a stranger,
he left at home for me this brush
made somehow from a badger.

I wonder now if that long-dead
animal would rather
I made use of what survives of him
or buried it near my father.

I wonder, dreamily shaving twice,
how were the hairy of England
supplied with brushes: were there millions
of badgers then on this island?

Some innocents must have groomed
their tender faces with terrier,
some aesthetes maybe with the straightened
curls of a famous whore.

I see the diploma'd shearers
of the Fur Artists' Guild,
their mediaeval rights, their training
in morgue and zoo and field.

I see the royal shops
full of brushes from the Empire,
gold handles carved by Cellini & Freud,
fledged with spider-legs or zebra.

And my poor father was stuck with badger!
I'm wondering what I'd choose,
when there's a bang at the door and a cry:
'Can we afford two loos? . . .'

Backs

They say (and don't They know?)
on everybody's spine there is a patch
you can't touch, above the wash
even of astronomical tides, where bugs may draw
their war-canoes up safely in the shade
of an aboriginal forest between our shoulder-blades,
a lost world where our mother's bacteria
live on preserved into this harsher era.

But no. It's short-armed men, importers of loofahs,
mounters of pumice and ivory hands on sticks,
who spread this tale. Behind our backs
there is no Eden where an old flea is safe:
there is no Terra Incognita on the body.
I know: I bent my left arm up today
to meet my right which angled over
and met it, and the myth gently exploded.

Watches

I wear my father's last but one
wristwatch, having broken my own.
Its crazed face, its wild cricketer's strap
always slipping off,
its inability to keep up
with the regular and not excessive

marching speed of the universe
explain his buying one of those self-winders:
he was a busy man
and couldn't afford the soft unclear
evaporation
of minutes, a day or two a year.

The busy man winds his watch on
as he drives, writes a prescription,
taps a sweating back.
But later, sitting for hours
rehearsing from his notebook
the names of French birds or Italian flowers,

he had to remember to keep
the watch from going to sleep,
swinging an arm over the side
of the blocky uncomfortable chair.
The first time the watch died
would have been a puzzle, then a small despair.

Later it would be worse: to realise
he could not give a watch its exercise.
So it ran down and somewhere waited
for the moment of moving on,
when watches are fastened to related
wrists, and time marks time again.

The Health of Houses

Taking a house to the dentist
may be imagined:
the path reeled in like a butterfly's tongue,
the drainpipes hitched to keep
a pair of basements up,
the windows already painfully clenched.

I see it stomping down the street
holding the owner's hand
with a blowing curtain,
docile at crossings but perhaps
hanging back at hardware shops
and the dirty plumber's surgical displays.

Our neighbour however kindly brings
the dentist in: Number Twenty-Five
turning its eyes to heaven
opens its doorway wide
and leans on our sympathetic wall:
we feel the terrible exploring drill,

shocking blows too near the heart
(what if that chisel slips?)
and the itchy addition of bypass pipes,
joints, bowls and knobs.
I think we are all too old for this –
both houses long for peace.

But soon discomforts, even pains,
are forgotten, and my house
will look down at me with reproach:
Can I not hear the vigorous flushing,
the joyful creak of showers?
It has new fittings: it'll want new glands.

1860

Sometimes the draught around the driver's seat
or past the kitchen radiator reaches
into my memory: among the bones
of my right leg I feel the shapeless fingers
straying that firmly grasped the teenage body
of my grandfather's brother Matthew, who one night
slept on the hill while herding sheep. The pain
in his hip next day went on and finished him.
It was the year of the high Victorian dream:
Great Expectations, and 'Mr Huxley, was it
your grandfather or your grandmother was an ape?'
– and this white pain, that lingers in *my* bones.

At Covent Garden in 1912

(January 15th)

My heroes nearly shook hands. Oedipus
called from his altar: 'Somebody come save us
and stop this pointed rain of illness.'

And Reinhardt sent down the aisles an enormous chorus
of Theban Citizens, hundreds I would guess
from the photos, and both sexes. In the crush

they carried to centre stage (not in Greek dress)
a struggling bald man of about seventy years.
Good Lord, it's Henry James, cursing his tardiness.

But they're singing: 'O sweetly spoken Word of Zeus . . .'
Quite a lot better than the rain of boos
he received last time. He looks up, amused.

August 24th Again

Around the edge of our formal
garden it was cool
under the portico roof.
The pangs of one who knows
he is not going to starve
tickled us pleasantly, like the claws of love.
We watched the plates on the table
fall in like a parade, in rows.

It was our last family meal.
A little dust can kill,
drifting in deep enough,
or gas the warm breeze blows.
We became holes in the earth,
trace-fossils of that day's uncertain self.
Now another kind of table
stands there, another kind of rose.

Latin-speaking but dirty-handed people
sit waiting, hungry. I swirl
among them, eager to serve
ancient invisible delicacies.
But then I observe
in the flowerbed lies a statue of myself,
and there arranged around the table
your ancestors' *imagines*:

Grandfather whom I can't recall,
Father with that incipient smile
even under the death-mask, never grave,
and Mother. Nothing that shows
your face or mine: we didn't have
a formal end – our clock was just turned off.
But there is little Sextus, on the table,
who led us to Hades, a nick out of his nose.

Miss Evans

She came in daily, looking a red-cheeked girl
of a Welsh peasant, twice as old as me,
with a charming smile and something of a smell.

She was reading every leaf of history
of Cardiganshire we had, for legal proof
that Henry the Eighth had cheated her family.

Soon she'd be taking Queen Elizabeth
to court: the abbey lands of Strata Florida
were hers, she would maintain till her last breath.

Meanwhile the Arab students liked to tease her
with false proposals: one full week she glowed
as a honeymoon in Paris loomed closer and closer,

and somehow painlessly evaporated
into her memories of a youth in Wales . . .
bathing in streams and rolling dry in meadows.

Still she kept coming, mistress of Close Rolls
and Feet of Fines and Household Books – somewhere
she'd find the evidence for her appeals.

We'd groan as she approached, with a Calendar
of still more Privy Papers she must see.
Yet what she brought us, smiling, was the odour
of Justice and the sanity of the country.

Sylvia and Me

Coincidences don't just happen,
they need helping –
take me and Sylvia for example.
We both get born in ports,
only a fortnight apart,
but the Atlantic separates
our doubtless identical cots.

After eight years her father
dies – 'abandons her forever',
as she puts it, calling him unfaithful.
That year my father too expelled
his eldest (and other children)
from Paradise (Liverpool) –
but I knew it was Hitler's fault.

Anyway – I cross the sea
(in the Year of the U-Boat Nineteen Forty)
and sit in the Boston hotel lobby,
waiting for Sylvia. Does she show?
Steal an hour from school? Heck, no.
She didn't even come and throw
a snowball at the English dope.

Some parallels would have turned away
at that; not ours. We both marry
people from Yorkshire (my
mother-in-law claimed to have given
Sylvia's husband a measles injection),
we both have two children.
But damn! We both leave London.

(I had a lovely sailing-dinghy,
bought from a man called Wijesinghe –
but couldn't take it inland with me.
I put an ad in the *New Statesman*
and sold it to a would-be boatman
called Horder, who gave me a rotten
cold to take home to Middle England.)

'Something' made me try again.
I dispatched a poem to the PEN
yearbook. Taken. She from Devon
sent two ('Candles' and 'You're'). The
PEN Club invited us to a party
somewhere on the King's Road, Chelsea.
Fall '62. We were both thirty.

Now we hear the silent cheer
of Coincidence: 'Sylvia –
this is Alistair.'
Our hands touched. A friendly creature
had said 'how much she wants to meet you' –
the social fire-extinguisher –
but she said nothing. She was not the editor,

but a separated wife.
Somehow I drifted off,
looking for George or Geoffrey.
She'll have stood still to survey
the roaring party surface
for Wevills and Merwins and Murphys
who had been her friends or rivals.

Coincidence was aghast –
all that geometry wasted!
She left the contributors' list
within months. So did MacNeice
and Roethke. The Yeatsian gas . . .
And now, thirty years later,
I learn her doctor's name was Horder.

The Not So Barefoot Contessa

After being divorced
for having more shoes than two centipedes,
she became the first
American countess
of a place not mentioned by Italian guides.
I once refused her a kiss.

Oh, what a scene she threw us!
To be rejected by a protégé
aged twelve (the brief non-kissing stage)
was worse for her than public lips for me.
Alone, we might have made a happier story –
I was not unmoved by her controlled rondures.

Reflecting now on us both,
I am astonished by her energy –
and lack of wrinkles, actually:
for, as someone afterwards said,
she spent all her life in bed
or else in some (nunlike, possibly) bath.

Is it ungrateful to write
in such cool terms of one who played
hostess after all
to three of Hitler's little targets?
As a matter of fact I think she might be glad
her performance lasts in anyone's recall.

For she had no say in what she 'gave'
and we as helplessly received.
That day we just forgot our parts
briefly, and showed
more than is usually allowed:
our unguarded breasts – our hearts.

Ned

The three letters of his name
suddenly resurrect him,
lounging on some horizon,
much like the long corpse of Christ
in Michelangelo's *Deposition*.

There was something ideal
about him: the naked male
of Greek stone, the Amazon
man about the jungle, face
and body matched, lone playboy in the sun –

Ned in his Jantzen swimwear
was spear-carrier as star.
He could speak, though. The word 'drawl'
comes back, loaded with distaste.
Someone must have thought his tongue lacked control.

Far from it, memoirs tell us,
picturing in a criss-cross
of brown and white the relief
of long beauty: Ned screwing
his opposite, Someone's ivory wife.

Breathing in America

Hal offered me a shower. What hospitality
I thought at the time: original
And absolutely right (I'd walked across
From Amsterdam); how personal
And yet American, to let me see
The secrets of his soapdish and the box

Where he stands naked and alive.
But I was overflowing with interpretations
Of everything then. Now I think
He might have been afraid his offprints
And Amy's heaped-up books might have
Bored me (far from it) or I just stank.

Anyway I was sitting cool and clean
Among the letters and lectures, bills and acts,
When their friend Robert Blue
Dropped in, with 'Hi! Relax!'
And Amy too. Their afternoon
For exercise. Their body-guru.

And this is where I really felt
Some boundary crossed, for as we lay
And thought, or lifted feet and hands
In that contented obedient way
Sensing the contents of our pelt,
I got lost in his commands:

I could no longer understand
'Inhale' (the chest goes out) and live.
'Exhale.' (The chest goes in!) The Latin
Began to choke me. I had the bends
From bubbling words, and had to dive
Back deeper, to breathe Anglo-Saxon.

Somewhere down there were the controls,
A place where something is beating
Untended, the place where George
The automatic pilot

Nudges his stick and levels off,
Below the tapping roots of language.

That was where I had to get,
Escaping from the whole exercise
Of words, now well over my head.
They must have thought I was just unfit,
But I had sunk to a paradise
Where nothing has yet been said,

Like the sequoia woods where sun
Slants down diagonal dusty rays
And a hummingbird is seen
High up among these luminous rafters
As of an unbuilt house.
There I lay and breathed again.

Leaving North Dakota

It was a small place
somewhere near Williston:
I nearly went off
the road from seeing
this echelon of cranes –
whoopers! – but aren't they extinct? –
swirling up in the river of air
over Trenton. Welcome!
welcome back!
                    I stopped at the store,
looked up the street. The floating
white wings edged with black
eddied past roofs, against
a thunderhead, out of sight.

Two little girls
arrived on a bike,
the younger, perched behind,
in a short dress like a tutu
and bright red tights
with holes in the heels.
Neither wore shoes.
I followed them into the store.
They offered their mother's grocery list
and a book of food-stamps,
and disappeared in the aisles.

I bought a chocolate milk
and left, again looking up
for the wild creatures
surviving in their niche.

A man on the train that night
told me, I think with malice,
my birds were pelicans.
As we picked up speed through Palermo,
and rattled on towards Surrey,
Norwich, Denbigh and Rugby,
the geographical center
of the whole continent,

56

I talked about the Indians
with this enormous bastard,
the kind of man I could never
meet anywhere else,
and thought of Johnson on Raasay
whispering to Boswell,
'This is the patriarchal life;
this is what we came to find.'
For this I left Grand Forks,
and all my delicate friends:

The rough grain of America!

At Mohammed V Airport, Casablanca

The dream of the living poet is
To be sold at aerodromes
Among the books about coitus,
Clothes, gardens and homes.

And here, where Miss Bergman said
Goodbye for ever to Bogart,
Is the place to be bought and read,
The perfect reward for our rogue art!

Then I saw four-square on the shelves
The *Roman de la Rose*
And Guillaume and Jean beside themselves
At beating all of us!

A Public Notice

Where is M.A.A. Khan
of Balliol, who owned
my Euripides III
(Oxford Classical Text,
Gilbertus Murray, *ed.*)
before me?

I was at Balliol
too, sort of, so often
I came to tea there with
X (well, we've quarrelled) that
I was in the college
photograph.

Mirza? . . . Mahmood? . . . Ali?
Akbar? Asfandyar?
who read only *Bacchae*,
but neatly noted down
meanings of hard phrases
in pencil.

After so many years
of not reading your book.
I suddenly wonder:
Are you the grandfather
in law of Jemima,
Imran's wife?

Did you see the play I
translated, *Medea*?
Miss Rigg was very good . . .
My dear chap, if you read
these odd verses, do write.
We could meet . . .

Anywhere! Pakistan?
Herat? Kashmir? Delhi?
Just give me an excuse
to follow my namesake
Alexander Magnus
to Asia!

The Art of Travel

After some days of feeling foreign
(anemia of the character,
an unexpressed where am I
and who's the Prime Minister)
they suddenly came to, in Florence.

She says it was in the Uffizi.
She had just seen Salome
with someone's head on an ashet
swimming in gravy, when he
hared off, crying out Well met!

to the King of Scotland, recognised
three centuries away.
Outside too became homey
when they glimpsed a dog, seen last
in the Adoration of the Magi.

They had thought it a dog of art,
the fantasy of a Martian
(called Sandy by some misnomer)
who had never seen a real one.
They saw the world could be Italian.

The Loss of Marbles

tantaene animis caelestibus irae?
      – Virgil, *Aeneid* I

Feeling our way along the coast, consulting
Book Three of the *Aeneid* in reverse,
we had left Etna floating in light airs
like a grass skirt projected on the blue vaulting
above Trinacria, and aimed for the famous white
Doric legs of the temple of Hera, which dance
unseen in the haze beyond Locri of the Epizephyrians –
a people we have longed for years to meet.

Late the next afternoon we approached the Cape
so ominously named in the singular now
'Colonna', and rocking in the gentle flow
of a north-set tide we cursed the devilish bishop
who stole the temple, sea-mark for millennia,
to build his palace, now itself a ruin.
O Stoics! we raged for Hera even in Croton,
moored to the mole, last home of her *colonne.*

In Corfu Harbour

for Peter and Joan

Ἐλευθέρα Κόρκυρα,
Χέζ' ὅπου θέλεις
*[it's free, it's Corcyra,
shit where you lie]*
Strabo, VII

Here I am, standing in a bow again
looking astern, the anchor and some chain
in my left hand, held out over the side,
ready for dropping . . .

        Forty years ago
landing in Porto Santo Stephano
I held the tiller, gave the word ('Let go')
to sails and anchor, drifted down stern first
and stepped ashore myself to make us fast,
manoeuvres done so often here you feel
the weight you're swinging isn't iron and steel
but a Homeric boulder and a rope:
the job is still to make the movement stop

before you hit the ground, let the boat ride
the water while you jump onto the sand
dryshod and with a weapon in one hand,
a stern-warp in the other.

        But today
the anchor bit too late, I hear you say.
I haul us back to where we were before
and free the anchor from the harbour floor.
(Captains are always right.) And now I wear
some Corfu muck across my chest, a smear
of classic human filth, the history
dropped by this old Corinthian colony
since it was founded (734 BC).

After, I clean the deck, the shirt, and me.

A Floater in the Aqueous Humour

It looks like two wheels with a cyclist bent
over them, and above his head an aerial
whipping about: it is the only real
thing I can see in the environment.
For the blank page dissolves, a blowing mist
under my hand: the mote
drifts away leftwards but
can be brought back (I turn my head) – and focused.

It hovers on my fingers as I write.
It runs away from the hand-lens. I insist,
but it is not enlarged. Since I began to watch,
one wheel has eaten the other, plus the cyclist.
Or has it turned end-on? I train my sight
on the swelling tyre: something's about to hatch –
a worm out of the apple of my eye?
or the soft dotting of an inner i?

It beats across the white field like the starved
aggressive creatures of computer games,
but I grow fond of it, empty as it seems
and friendless – or, since I must be its friend,
uncared for. It's gone unobserved,
though seen, across my world and life
perhaps for years. Only today I give
my whole mind to this shining ampersand.

Nobody else can see it, and the heart
its jerks must represent is mine, I guess.
It seems to float out there, but it's a part
of my most precious and protected space –
washing across this window, back and forth,
altering slightly all my images –
and tacking round its globe still when the eyes
themselves have turned and face my father's blindness.

Two Poems For J.M.

On the Last Day of 1993

You gave me the beautiful
notebook. It is like a bowl
a helping of food would spoil.

I guess you couldn't bear to write
on its rag pages. It was uncut
and I guess you managed to open it,

but were overcome by its perfection.
It looks finished now. I shall have to begin
by mis-spelling my name on page l,

and then more gently persevere
word by word, smear by smear,
till it's worn, obscure, and dear.

But it chose a good year to come:
In spring I sail to Byzantium.

Finishing the Notebook

Jimmy, two years ago you gave me this
notebook; and now I could return it full
you're dead, and writing to you is unreal.
I am addressing yesterday's clouds, for business
goes on without you.
                    But your new book came,
as if to tease me: I'll be in a file
on somebody's computer, and I smile
suddenly seeing you can play the game
onesidedly – as when you were alive
in fact – with poems hidden in your shroud
generously sent, old love-codes read aloud
for the first time to old friends who survive.
And we can't answer, with applause or hisses:
your poems get better and better; we can't be heard,
but you keep on pronouncing a fresh last word.
We are reduced to blowing the wind kisses.

Learning Spanish

for Caroline

A dictionary my slow paintbox, I step out,
tipping-in objects, through Cervantes-land,
at roughly the pace of the pen in his thinking-hand.
For as *Alforja* becomes a saddlebag
before my eyes, I think I see his thought
touching it like a shadow: the stitched skin
seen but not mentioned here conceives an onion,
to be born later, on a hungrier page.

A writer's landscape, like an unfinished one
by Edward Lear, has blanks – with perhaps 'gamboge'
or 'misery' scrawled across an odd-shaped patch
in the middle, for the reader to complete.
The book is everyone's: his, yours, even mine –
Sancho rides through it *como un patriarca*
and my inner painter flashes an altar-picture
which I paste neatly in beside the knight.

Feeling my way, I think I touch the grain
and edge of Spanish things as he did, groping
through the dark mind along the story-rope.
As he picks out and plays a word, I feel,
striking them *a soslayo*, the morning sun
of their first day together. The light is not in
their eyes – he's faced them north. We see the unwritten
country beyond his fist, becoming real.

One ink-drop made those mountains I once saw
from the ocean sailing south. Another drop
was teased to form a second-hand book-shop
in a bazaar I hope one day to see,
in a city full of houses with tiled floors
and armchairs all of wood where Sancho's sons
and daughters read – and look up what he means
in their own Spanish–Spanish dictionary.

Facing South

for Tony Harrison

Happiness, therefore, must be some form of theoria.
— Aristotle, *Nicomachean Ethics*, X,8

Theoria: . . . a looking at, viewing, beholding . . . 'to go
abroad to see the world' (Herodotus) . . . 2. of the mind,
contemplation, speculation, philosophic reasoning . . . theory . . .
II. the being a spectator at the theatre or the games . . .
— Liddell & Scott, *A Greek-English Lexicon*

Sat at my desk, I face the way I would
migrate: sunwards along this cobbled lane,
over the poplar trees of Elmfield Road,
across the Town Moor, up the mud-grey Tyne,
screaming with other swifts along the spine
of man-made England, eating airy food
and dozing in slow circles over Spain . . .
to the great desert where they still wear woad.

I had to buy an Apollo window-blind
to shut that out – the interesting sky
pours vagueness into the unresting mind
more than the prettiest-coloured passer-by,
more than the cars mysteriously left
unlocked by jolly women and dour men –
so many people unafraid of theft –
I have to watch till they come back again.

I never saw a thief here. The one thing
that pricks our quiet bubble is the roar
of comment from St James's – the fans sing
inaudibly, but bellow when we score.
Horror seems far away: our car-alarms
play the continuo of crime; we feel
the needles hovering near our neighbours' arms;
the viruses float in; but peace is real.

We suffer some illusion of control
in watching: so, the passenger keeps the car
safe if she watches the white line unroll;
the watching fans 'support' the football star;

66

watching the world wag past our café chair
gives us a sense of ownership: we share
some of that passing chic or savoir faire,
forgetting we are only who we are.

I must shut all that out. I want to make
these verbal systems in my workshop here.
Watching the world's a job too big to take:
I want to make small worlds that will cohere.
We have both travelled: south, east, west. I go
north now, quite near, where on the first of May
our earth relaxes and its rivers flow:
there I want nothing but to stay, and stay.

I could fly further; I've been free for years,
but don't migrate, for always there outside
in all the infinite other hemispheres
there'd be more sights from which I'd have to hide:
I'd have to take the blind, to blot out views
that would distract the wandering inner sight,
that pleasure Aristotle says we choose:
the blank I look at as I sit and write.

Aerea

IN THE FORESTS OF MANHATTAN

EMMANUEL HOCQUARD

AEREA

IN THE FORESTS OF MANHATTAN

TRANSLATED BY LYDIA DAVIS

THE MARLBORO PRESS

First English-language edition.

Copyright 1992 The Marlboro Press, Marlboro, Vermont.

Translation copyright 1992 by Lydia Davis

Originally published in French under the title
AEREA DANS LES FORÊTS DE MANHATTAN
Copyright P.O.L. Éditeur, 1985

The publication of the present volume has been made possible
in part by a grant from the National Endowment for the Arts.
The costs of translation have been met in part by a subvention
from the French Ministry of Culture.

Manufactured in the United States of America

Library of Congress Catalog Card Number 92-60853

Clothbound edition: ISBN 0-910395-88-8
Paperbound edition: ISBN 0-910395-89-6

TABLE OF CONTENTS

Aerea

IN THE FORESTS OF MANHATTAN

I. ZACHARIE

I will have no descendants.

Black, motionless on the ground in the middle of the road, the scorpion aimed its shining stinger at me in the soft light of dusk. However futile its warlike display may have been, however puny its anger at the approach of my white soles, I too became motionless before it and for a long time observed this frightened, melancholy figure that was barring my way. Yes, I stayed there, a few steps from the scorpion, until its fear had insinuated itself into me just as surely as its venom would have, until its tormented form had engraved its coaly sign upon the heart of the child I was.

And I turned back. Yes, I turned back, that day, for the first time.

Sitting today at my long table, before the open window that looks out on the trees, my gaze lost in the dense foliage, I let my thoughts slip noiselessly along with the great white clouds of the end of summer. Mingling with the rustle of the leaves in the wind is the uninterrupted purring of the air conditioner's transformer, an enormous concrete block bristling with open metalwork before which David is parking the little orange bus.

Dear David, who rents out his services as chauffeur to pay for his ornithology studies, always even-tempered, even last night coming back from an outing on the Mississippi, smiling in the midst of the shouts of his drunken passengers and agreeing to make a detour, at one o'clock in the morning, down a bumpy road across the corn fields in search of a case of beer in a drugstore he knew.

Observing his face by the light of the dials on the dashboard, I suddenly thought that his unchanging smile boded no good. But once again I was mistaken. Whistling to himself in the night at the wheel of his little bus, David was thinking of nothing but the singing of the birds he goes to study every Sunday, in the fields and woods, in the company of his friend Jessica, his beautiful friend with the green eyes, an expert in Medieval French.

"Yes, Adam," Aerea said to me, the obstacle is the language!"

I was standing in a large room, over against the wall, looking at the sparkling gown spread out at my feet over the entire surface of the parquet. Aerea came in.

"Here," I said to her, "is your wedding dress."

She gave me a radiant look and, putting her hand in mine, contemplated with delight the long embroidered train on which was repeated as far as the eye could see an iridescent pattern of blue feathers like those in ancient Egyptian tomb paintings. Then she moved away without a word and left the room by a secret door I hadn't noticed.

"Well, that's a very nice dream, Adam," she said to me the next day with the same expression of surprise and joy I had seen on her face in the dream as she looked at the sumptuous dress. "Isn't that royal train a good omen?"

Not long after that, she walked out of my life the same way she had walked out of my dream.

Aerea's name might have appeared next to mine on the last page of the genealogical tree. Yes, I would have been proud to add her name in my small handwriting, like the tenderest of promises, on that last page where mine was inscribed on the day of my birth forty years ago. But the little flame-shaped inset contains only the letters of the word Adam, my name, the only sign of life henceforth in the whole of that great extinct mass of foliage.

Now that the bonds have been loosened, now that Aerea has left me, with her white retinue of Asias and Oceanias, I remain alone before the dry tree whose leaves will never bear other names. Now I can dream. And my blue-tinged dream is no longer disturbed except by brief, rare turbulences of memory that quickly abate and leave no traces behind them.

In a room on the second floor of the Museum of Natural History, David took me over to a lead cabinet. When he opened its door, a strong smell of naphthalene wafted forth. Smiling, he lifted out of a shallow drawer, from among many rows of hummingbirds, a precious specimen whose minuscule, stiff body he turned delicately between his fingers. He pointed out to me the blue plumage on the top of the head and the breast of the dead bird, of the same mottled blue as the wedding train in my dream.

"This one," he explained to me proudly, "belongs to a variety formerly very sought after by the Incas for their funeral adornments."

But, reader, perhaps you don't like birds? Perhaps you think they bring unhappiness? Don't worry: no birds live in my memories. Not a single one.

Night has fallen on the trees and on the great plains of the middle of the world. As I listen to the icecubes clink in my glass, I admire the delicate nudity of my smooth-bodied companion, Eve by Cranach the Younger.

"Language is clothing, Aerea," I answered, brushing her lips with my fingertips. "There isn't any obstacle, not the slightest obstacle. Whoever said Adam and Eve talked to each other in paradise?"

Her eyes, gazing down at the blade of the silver knife, shone with contained anger and her gleaming teeth imprinted their precise mark on the buttered rusk that she laid down on the table where we were having breakfast. Behind my dark glasses I watched her fingers with their translucent nails dance among the glimmers of the cups and silverware, I watched her thick hair falling in waves over her shoulders, the white fabric of her nightshirt stretching over her chest.

"You're not funny, Adam. Not in the least funny!"

I watched as her beautiful pale lips moved. My eye was hurting me.

Imagine, reader, Ulysses far away from his own people, on a hot afternoon in early summer, in the American countryside next to the ocean, his right eye closed by an abcess and wax in his ears. You will be able to form a fair idea of me.

Lying on my bed, I was looking out through the open door of my wood cabin, watching the rain fall. I could see only the gray sky and the warm rain falling on the grass. Burning with fever on top of the sheet, not thinking very well, for moments at a time I would sink into a heavy somnolence in which ancient smells would assault me: baths of dye, lime, mulberries crushed on the ground.

Soon I saw the two forms advancing slowly in the distance: Aerea and Zacharie walking hand in hand, entirely absorbed in an intimate conversation, he watching where he put his little feet, she careful to measure her steps to his. I saw them advance peacefully toward me through the wet grass.

Zacharie considered me without saying anything. Then, looking at Aerea:

"Why doesn't he talk?" he asked in his plaintive voice.

"He comes from very far away, Zac, from the other side of the ocean. He speaks a language you can't understand."

"Is he going to die?"

"He's resting because he's sick. That's why we're leaving again tomorrow. He has to see a doctor."

Everything is quiet. Everything is abnormally quiet in the night. Sitting on my narrow iron bed, my eyes wide open in the darkness, I listen. Outside, the purring of the transformer has stopped. I stand up and look out the window. David's little bus isn't there any longer.

Aerea was doing her nails in the next room, standing in front of the window. Motionless, her head bowed, her hair pulled back to one side, she was wearing only her little pale blue stretch panties, which the mirror reflected back to me as a spot of brightness.

"Adam," she said to me as she applied the polish to her nails, "when are you going to decide to grow up?"

It wasn't a question, of course, and the indulgent kindness in her voice wasn't addressed to me.

The day before, I had given her a pair of earrings made of translucent red stone. Each stone was in the form of a teardrop. When Aerea had opened the small tissue paper bag, one of the earrings had fallen to the floor and broken. She had said that she could glue it back together with nailpolish, something she had learned to do in college. Then she had scolded me rather vehemently for my irresponsibility: instead of going to the doctor, hadn't I strolled up and down Lexington Avenue so that I could bring these earrings back to her?

Without answering, I watched her in the mirror. My eye was hurting me, and in the smell of nailpolish that floated between us, I thought of Zacharie again, a little angel naked and wan under the summer rain, warning me twice over in his nasal peacock screech: "Go away! Go away!"

"He went to study a migration," Jessica told me over the phone. "Be a nice guy, Adam, come pick me up tonight and take me to the pool. That will get you out, for once, away from your papers and your books."

After putting a log on the fire, the first fire of the season, David poured more wine into Jessica's glass and mine; then he sat facing us on the white wool carpet, his back to the fireplace.

"Imagine very low walls in curved lines, and grass everywhere as yellow as straw. Squat trees whose gray branches all bear dry leaves bleached by the light, shining and rustling as though they were made of tin. That's the whole landscape. A few flowers the color of coagulated blood and their thin leaves as wrinkled as paper ash. No children, no domestic animals. Not one woman. No voices, no smells. In the center of town, the only sign of life is the sound of cars passing endlessly.

"There exist enormous areas where my fellow countrymen, descendants of the pioneers who came in their old wagons, haven't even set foot yet. They live in their long, silent cars a few inches off the ground. The real encounter between the country and its inhabitants hasn't taken place yet.

"You're an odd fellow, Adam, and I'm sure you would be sensitive to the gloomy charm of these no-man's-lands where a label from a bottle of Mexican beer shines in the sun like a pool of molten gold among the little mummified flowers, and where the trees, permanently withered, are used once a year as perches for migrating birds. Some day you'll see it, friend. But you won't see the Indians. No, you won't see them."

David's voice, as he spoke, was warm and indolent. In the flickering light of the wood fire, he smiled, his head inclined, his eyelids swollen as though he had missed a few hours of sleep, he wrapped us, Jessica and me, in his invariably kind smile.

"Here, it's different. Here, we're proud of our autumns, the most beautiful in the continent. You'll see. How lucky you are to have come at this time of the year!"

"We have to go out. We have to go out now. Afterwards, it'll be too late."

All night long, the air conditioner had fought relatively successfully against the crushing heat, outdoors, of the New York summer. The album of nudes—*Women Photographed by Women*—wedged in the window to block an air hole had served its temporary purpose after a fashion and when the first glimmers of dawn found their way into the little apartment on 86th Street, I got up and opened the window of the next room. An unexpected coolness entered the space and filled me with a vast sense of well-being.

Surrounded by smells of perfumes and scattered dresses, the abandoned bed loomed as a milky rectangle in the dim light; on the inner sill of the open window I recognized from their small handwriting my letters to Aerea thrown in a heap out of their envelopes, the ones on top spotted by rain and already covered in dust. Alone among the perfumes and the dresses, I stood still in that inhabited room, delighting for a long time in the coolness on my face and hands.

In the other room, Aerea was asleep, lying on the large purple rug in front of the brick fireplace where the brass tips of the andirons gleamed among the ferns. Recumbant under the mirror, she was shrouded in the folds of the white sheet; her heavy hair fell in a dark wave to the floor; one of her hands lay outside the sheet, a single hand in the half-light.

"Aerea," I called to her softly in her sleep, "we have to go out right away, before the heat becomes overwhelming again."

Now that everything is over, now that the white net of Aerea's silence has fallen on me in answer to my own silence, I spend whole days looking at the leaves that autumn is already clouding with its silky hues behind the pane of my panoramic window. Yes, I look endlessly at the deep tossing and waving of these threatened leaves,

in which I discover more than one restless echo of my life,
presently without employment.

"What thoughts are they, Aerea, that make you more
desirable every day?"

"Do me a favor," she answered in her melodious voice.
"Tonight, go sleep in the bed or on the couch but not
with me. You look like death again today and I will never
sleep with a dead man."

Wrapped in the white sheet, a gold bracelet on her
wrist, Aerea was sleeping on the large purple rug while
the little air conditioning factory filled the space of the
night with a din as vast and resonant as the noise of the
ocean.

The day the first leaves loosed their hold on the branches,
fluttering down before my closed window, I was visited
by my friend Sokrat. The capricious flight of the dead
leaves, the light, soundless tumble of their dismal little
wings dancing before my eyes in the transparency of the
air, was echoed at my back—the rather bowed back of the
middle-aged man that I am—by the arpeggio of precise
little raps dealt to the front door by my very thin and very
near-sighted Turkish friend.

"Obviously, Adam," he said to me gravely, setting his

glass down on my polished table, "obviously you're not in the least Mediterranean."

A disapproving tsk-tsk of his tongue against his teeth issued from his full-lipped mouth; from behind his thick-lensed glasses his byzantine gaze went back and forth several times between Cranach the Younger's Eve, my gentle high-breasted companion, and the vast window behind which the branches were stirring under a rain of golden leaves.

"You're ill, I'm worried about you. Do you know the great abandoned palaces falling into ruin on the banks of the Bosporus? Majestic and cold, there by the waterside, they look as though the only thing holding them up now were their reflections. You're one of them, Adam. Aesthetics, my friend, will do you in more quickly and more surely than alcohol or the shafts of your disastrous loves! For you, beauty will prove fatal, and I see clearly that what draws you to it is death. So let's drink to our friendship and to your beautiful death, but don't ever try to tell me you're Mediterranean again."

Blowing the white smoke of my cigarette toward the window, I listened to what my sententious friend was saying but never lost sight of the little grove of trees struggling against the autumn in the kaleidoscope of my watchful glances. For my patience, watching and waiting, is fully equal to David's. But then, who knows? Who knows?

I have always been a sort of altruist. Naturally, with the passage of time, and as I have gained confidence, my altruism has changed. It has been many years, by now, since I stopped approaching other people in search of affection and gratitude, my arms loaded with offerings and my heart overflowing with lofty sentiments. But despite appearances, my disinterestedness has not turned into lack of interest nor my indifference into coldness. My altruism has assumed new forms.

"You're a good person, Adam, but you don't see things face on. I would never be able to marry a man who was satisfied with so few words and so few ideas."

"Aerea," I answered, looking tenderly at her out of my healthy eye, "isn't that the best sort of pledge for a beginning?"

These days, all my altruism goes into the way I look at what is around me.

Under the pale trees in the starry night, all the windows of the house were illuminated. Through the wide open door, the light from the chandeliers made the dead leaves shine as they crackled under my feet.

In the center of the vast ground-floor room, the largest room in the beautiful house which was falling into ruin inside, as was evinced by the cracks in the walls and the ceiling, one long table was cluttered with cosmetics, makeup and multicolored spangles, another with a jumble of clothes, moth-eaten theater costumes, tattered wigs and masks, a third with bottles of beer, jars of sour pickles, plates of sweet bread and roast turkey. Making its way among these tables, a fat siamese cat stopped in front of the people who had been eating and who were now still busy putting on disguises and making up their faces, preened himself and mewed hoarsely, begging for a piece of the bird. From time to time, the dwarfish forms of children dressed up as husbands and wives would appear framed in the front doorway; their faces blackened, they would arrogantly call out "trick or treat," and as soon as someone threw them a coin or a handful of sweets would immediately disappear into the night like a flight of harpies. I watched as a group of young women bustled about the large table, carefully disfiguring themselves with strokes of their pencils and brushes. They were laughing so wholeheartedly, they seemed so happy with their sad metamorphoses that I too began to laugh. Taking my gaiety for approval, they tried to seize hold of me and paint my face with gaudy colors. I managed to slip away into the next room, where a large fire was burning in the fireplace.

In a dark suit, a white shirt, and a tie, his blond hair dyed black, his face powdered, his eyes ringed with a line of charcoal and his lips painted blood red, David was warmly welcoming his guests.

"David," I said, going up to him, "you look exactly like a sick penguin."

"Tradition, Adam, tradition," he answered. "Now go on and find Jessica. She's waiting for you."

With difficulty I made my way among the guests. Sitting on the couch, her dark hair cut short, wearing an elegant black openwork dress, Jessica was talking to two masked men. She and I were the only members of this comical assemblage not wearing makeup.

When she saw me coming toward her, when our eyes met in the soft light of this part of the room, her very green eyes, her strange and very beautiful green eyes shone and her serious face brightened with a calm smile.

"Stay with me," she said quietly. "This evening the two of us will talk French together."

Late in the night the muffled din of the festival of dead people and idiots echoed into the far distance. Late in the starry autumn night the debauchery continued; the houses decorated with cardboard skeletons were open to the spirits of the dead and to the masquerade of the living.

"Sokrat, my friend, even given your morbid penchant for sunsets, this winding river, this green river with its pink reflections right here under your windows, is an alarming spectacle that will end up corrupting your taste for good."

"My dear man," answered my Turkish friend, sighing, "this river is in every way wonderful and your morose spirit will not succeed in diminishing the pleasure I get, every day, from studying it. For the love of God, Adam, how do you manage to be so completely without any sense of poetry?"

The string of sadness has vibrated again on my tuneful lyre, breaking the harmonious accord between the taciturn watchman and the fall of the leaves in the light. Last night, Aerea appeared to me in a dream. She was sobbing.

The sky was white. The trees had no more leaves on them. Jessica's bluejeans were the last remaining patch of light in the landscape. Her knees parted in the pine needles, Jessica was sitting back on her heels, her hands laid flat on the tight material of her blue pants. She was smiling, her eyes closed. The breeze was moving a short lock of dark hair over her forehead. Standing, leaning against a tree, David was blowing gaily into his broad cupped hands and letting his eyes roam far away over the sparkling waters of the river. Shrewd observer, I felt the silence that followed Jessica's words expand and stretch like a soft material over the shape of a body. Under the early winter's morning sky, the three of us composed a perfect figure. The little beach we had chosen for our peaceful excursion was as hospitable as Corcyra's shore.

"There exists," said David, "a secret relationship, an immutable, stubborn pact between the natives and the powerful brown god. Invisible and omnipresent, the Mississippi plays a role in the lives of these stock breeders and farmers even more crucial than the dome of the Capitol or the Constitution. From the river, which flows in their hearts, they draw their unshakable faith in the legitimacy of their possessions. The "Father of all Waters" is the bank where their capital of memory prospers, their memory which, like money, like merchandise, like land,

The Marlboro Press is an independent publisher of serious literature: works of fiction, of intellectual history and philosophic travel, biography, chronicles, essays—a good many of them in translation.

If you have found this book of particular interest you may wish to know what others have appeared on our list and are forthcoming. We will be happy to send you a catalogue, and to answer any queries you may have.

Name

Street or box number

City

State   Zip

T M P

THE MARLBORO PRESS

P. O. BOX 157

MARLBORO, VERMONT 05344

bears fruit and is purified in its muddy waters. Now you and I, Adam, are Hottentots unconcerned by the old quarrel over precedence between Cain's and Abel's descendants. Too circumspect to believe in healing springs, we like unpredictable torrents, mushrooms, clouds. Picking and gathering is our mode of production. When your attentive gaze happens to fall abruptly on a bronzed boletus at the foot of a stump or in a patch of dead leaves, though obviously nothing was hiding it, what an ineffable encounter, Adam! To express it, analogy isn't much help at all, because words bloom too late. It's as though this object, suddenly there at your feet in its unblemished necessity and its tender sexual compactness, had come into being through the aleatory virtue of one of your fleeting looks. Born of a look, as of a lightning bolt! Such an abrupt birth, such a violent initial silence can only result in a great burst of laughter. God's laughter when he sees Adam for the first time, the divine laughter, unexampled, endless, whose crystalline echoes reverberate their perpetual harmony through the Universe. Believe me, the speculations of the farmers, of the inseminators, of the philosophers are only hollow, nostalgic counterfeits, vain attempts at appropriation. Isn't it pleasant to think what good disciples we are, at this moment, of the naked monk of Assisi?"

Jessica was the first to notice it. Almost motionless above the dark lace of the bare branches, the light trapezoid of yellow silk rose slowly into the sky.

"Oh! Look at it, Adam! Isn't it graceful?"

As though in response to Jessica's exclamation, the airy armature was shaken by little quivers as it tried to mount freely into the sky. But from the other side of the trees an invisible hand was holding onto the connecting string and the kite undulated with yellow shimmers and then obediently lay back in the brisk air until it was no more than a slender oblique line, to our eyes. And it bucked again; now, a translucent shield, it raised its loving mythological form above our heads; now, on our silent beach, another perfect triangle took shape, its celestial peak the pale silk structure rising through the void while between the water and the trees Jessica had come up to me. She had put her arm around my waist, she had slipped her hand under the cloth of my shirt; as we continued to stare at the apparition, I felt against my ribs the soft, imperious pressure of her breast.

"Adam," Aerea said to me, "we have to make love. That's the cure."

Since the dark green door of the large house had remained shut despite my calls, I decided to walk around the property. The evening was fine, the sky pink and, under my thin soles, the ground delightfully springy. I had entered the sunken path that went along the wall of the lower garden when I noticed a low structure that I didn't recognize, a simple cube of packed earth without door or windows, surmounted by a terrace in the center of which was the only means of access to the interior of the house, a square opening, open to the sky. Without hesitating, I hoisted myself up onto this terrace, slipped into the hole, and climbed down a ladder into a room situated below the level of the ground. This room, of pleasant dimensions, was furnished with meticulous care and gently lit by lamps. A low bed was covered with light-colored furs; the shimmering hues of the cushions and Oriental rugs added to the comfort and intimacy of the place.

As I gazed around, I was filled with an immense sense of repose: I was certain, at that moment, that my wandering had come to an end and that here, henceforth, nothing would ever come to disturb my serenity.

"Adam," Aerea said to me in her melodious voice, "what pleasure do you get out of describing so complacently what is in fact obviously your own grave? You have just proved yet again your incapacity for living; this kind of talk isn't very agreeable at breakfast!"

The dream house beneath the earth is certainly not my grave and my incapacity for living is surely no greater than Aerea's refusal to love or be loved.

"Little sister of Minerva," I answered her, "why do you persist in seeing my grave in your femininity? It was a happy dream, after all. Yet it will all end up dissolving in tears. And what will happen to the tears is what happens to glass in the earth: no more transparency, no more reflections, but color. A beautiful rainbow underground, Aerea, little iridescent flasks full of tears."

There has always been a bounding strength lying asleep in me. Sitting on my narrow iron bed, my mind alert in the darkness, I stay awake. I have become a lover of the night.

"And so Adam is leaving us. He's running away to the West."

Sokrat, already slightly drunk, was sitting cross-legged near the fire. The reflection of the flames in his thick glasses gave him the expression of a devilish jack-in-the-box. "Don't worry," David answered him with his usual good humor, "like all migrators he'll be back some day."

"Adam, don't listen to Sokrat," Jessica said to me, taking my arm. "Even though it isn't really like him, our friend feels sad when he thinks of tomorrow. Let's leave him to drink away his sorrow and go out for some air. Do you want to?"

Snow was falling in the night. The first snow of the year had begun falling the night before I was to leave. It had already covered the road and the underbrush; the darkness before us was streaked by the slow fall of the flakes. Her hands resting on the wooden balustrade, Jessica was silent; her fur collar now and then caught a pale flake of snow, downy as a ball of mimosa. Between the icy shadow of the little forest and the lit windows of the house from which bursts of muffled laughter came to us, we did not dare either move or talk, both of us absorbed in the immensity of the silence and tacitly wanting to preserve its inert emptiness.

"They're coming! Listen!" Jessica murmured.

I too had heard the noise inside the house. I had seen the two shadows move behind the windows. Now they were approaching the door we had closed behind us when we came out. I seized Jessica by the hand. With one leap I pulled her to the bottom of the porch steps and we began running over the slippery road, pursued by David and Sokrat.

"It's a kidnapping, David! That man has just kidnapped her!" shouted Sokrat in his sepulchral voice. "Catch up with them! Catch up with them!"

"Whatever you do, don't turn around, Jessica," I said to her in one breath. "The very sight of that Turk would turn you into a statue of ice!"

Without letting go of my hand, Jessica ran as fast as she could in her delicate shoes, in the snow that was swirling in front of her face. We ran without stopping as far as the transformer. When we stopped, all out of breath, we realized that our pursuers had given up the chase. First we saw our soft footprints intermingled in the fresh snow; then farther, very far away by the side of the white road, David's form bending over Sokrat, whom he was helping to stand up. We watched them move away; David was supporting Sokrat, who was staggering. Long after they had disappeared into the dark cool of the night, their joyful laughter echoed under the trees.

"How cheerful they are!" Jessica said with a faint smile, pressing my hand against her beating heart. "Will we be able to be as cheerful as that? Truly?"

23

When she opened her eyes again in the happy half-light, the yellow candle was still burning in front of my large window, which looked out on the night. The dancing flame cast its soothing gleams over her face and her body lying next to mine. Outside, the snow had stopped falling.

"Adam," she said, raising herself on one elbow and caressing my shoulder, "I'm the one who's going to leave now. Tomorrow morning the weather will be beautiful. David will drive you to the airport. Do you know what he'll say when he comes to get you?"

" 'Adam,' he'll say, 'I didn't have the heart to wake Jessica. She was sleeping so soundly and she hates good-byes.' And then he'll say: 'How lucky you are to be leaving for San Francisco at this time of year!' "

The snow was sparkling all around. The cold was intense and the key refused to turn in the frozen lock. Jessica walked around the little bus and without any difficulty removed the rear window. Her delicate body disappeared from my sight into the rectangular black opening. Through the frost-covered windows, I made out for the last time her graceful form slipping to the front of the vehicle in which David would take me away the next morning.

It wasn't the smell of the orange trees or the flowering mimosas, or even the antique odor of the familiar eucalyptuses, but the perfume of the myrtle, suddenly, in the damp shadow of the white walls. The morning was misty;

the sun hadn't yet dissipated the fog in the bay. Yes, first it was that, the smell of the myrtle, still green, the smell of Venus's shrub, that tore apart the mist, vibrating in the air like a powerful chord of brasses; immediately after, but only then, the very high, very pale pink curve in the diaphanous sky, the gentle concave line of the first bundle of metal cables. Such was, as I walked through the mist, my first sight of the bridge.

"Adam," said Aerea as she cleared the table where we had had our breakfast, "I wouldn't mind knowing something about your life before we met. Even though you talked in your sleep again last night, you don't seem to have any past or any memory. How could I marry a man whose feet are so rarely on the ground? I couldn't! Yesterday you didn't say a word all day. The fact is, you don't need anyone."

The yellow bunches of mimosa brushed against my face, the earth was ·fragrant under my feet, the bridge grew larger little by little to the rhythm of my slow approach, the pink of the roadway and the towers reddened; behind the suspended structure, I now made out the first waters of the Pacific.

"Now you have reached the end of the world. And yet this bridge thrown up over the ocean can't lead you anywhere."

And even so, yes, I set out to cross it. I walked for a long time on the bridge, which vibrated between the sky and water with all the cables of its red harp. For a long time I advanced between the vertical cables. I stopped in the middle of the bridge, midway between the two giant towers; leaning my elbows on the iron guard rail, I noticed below me a little freighter reentering the bay. Its engine was hiccuping, it was heeling over and seemed so defeated, rusting all over, that it looked as though it had survived some terrible storm. Was it the sight of that woebegone ship that made me decide abruptly to retrace my steps? In any case, I did turn back. Yes, once more I turned back. In the bluish fog, I again felt the rhythm of my steps fall into harmony with the long unwinding of my meditation on my life.

On my life?

II. THE RAINBOW DANCE

W hile I was asleep, the snow came down again. By early morning, it had obliterated every trace of the tires of the little frost-covered bus behind the wheel of which Jessica, a few hours earlier, had disappeared into the night after leaving me. I was ready to go, my bags deposited in the front hall. While waiting for David, who was supposed to drive me to the airport, I had walked outside to stretch my legs.

It was then that I saw the two sets of prints in the layer of fresh snow at the base of the transformer, those of the bird and those of the cat, intertwined at my feet like initials embroidered on a sheet. Had the bird landed on the snowy ground and hopped about after the cat had gone by? Or had the cat arrived after the bird had flown off? However it may have been, they had apparently not met: I didn't notice the least sign of a struggle or precipitous flight. No spot of blood, no lost feather. Nothing, on the surface of the snow, but the precise, delicate tracery formed by their double set of prints. Nothing but the light marks of the dance they had performed in this place, each absent for the other, both absent for me.

"Here's an amusing example of time frozen in space," I said to myself.

When I described what I had found to David, he merely nodded, continuing to stare out ahead of us through the clouded windshield at the icy road.

The day I saw them, those dreary wastelands of Albuquerque scattered with mummified flowers, I sent David a postcard showing a local festival: dancing Indians brandishing above their feather-coiffed heads cardboard crescents depicting, painted in strong colors, the seven bands of the rainbow.

After each of my trips, I have returned to my old place under the lamp. Again this evening my iridescent memory is clear, transparent like the icecubes that clink in my glass. Again this evening my typewriter's motor will purr as softly as the bellows of a little organ inlaid with mother-of-pearl leaf-work. Under my caressing fingers, the keys on the keyboard will be as smooth as ivory. Once again, sitting before the nudity of my insouciant companion,

Cranach the Younger's Eve, I will hear rising in me the song of those who accompanied my quests and my dreams.

For a long time now, my eyes have not been able to see them. Nor my hands touch them. Nevertheless, when a happy drunkenness overcomes me, I see them again—those who knew each other and those who never met—dancing in the prism of my memories. Then each of them seems to me like one nuance of the specter that I am.

David, Zacharie, Jessica, Sokrat, June, Médé, Montalban, Virginie, Remedios, Juan, Rosita. . . The crisscrossed letters of their names feed the fires of a sparkling alphabet that burns under the sign of Aerea, goddess of the woods, of hunting, and of fishing.

III. ON THE BRIDGE

His eyes lowered behind his shining glasses, Sokrat studied the game of goose set out between us. We were alone on the terrace of the open-air cafe, face to face at a table under the spring leaves. We were alone at that hour, still morning, occupied by our daily match under the trees with their newly limed trunks, away from the bursts of voices from the streets and the din of the cars.

"I've noticed that you don't change, Adam. You remain a prisoner of your images. Nothing distracts you from the incessant coming and going that tosses you back and forth among them."

Below our cafe under the trees, on the slopes of the uncultivated land sheets were drying in the wind, and from the Golden Horn plumes of black smoke rose into the sky. In the distance, between the minarets and the domes of the ash-colored city, the Sea of Marmara spark-led in the sun.

I threw the dice and made my move.

"Look, Sokrat, the first square shows a garden and the last a flowering grove with a goose resting in it. But a great many obstacles present themselves before one can reach it."

"Of course, Adam, of course. But what do you know about the hand that throws the dice? What do you know about it?"

Through the slender branches, the sun speckled the red cloth covering the table.

"The hand that throws the dice is the actual hand of the player. That's what I say about it."

Sokrat nodded.

"Oh, if only that thought would help you drive away the dark moods I so often see you slip into! How happy I would be for you!"

"But Sokrat," I retorted, "aren't I an agreeable play-mate? And," I added after a silence, "what do I have to complain about today? The memory of Aerea is fading."

"Who's talking about forgetting, Adam? On the con-trary—if only you wouldn't resort to such a feeble trick!"

Sokrat pouted disdainfully as he said these words, hammering his finger on the cloth as the wood of the little table under it reverberated.

"Every morning when I get here," I went on, trying to create a diversion, "the waiter hurries up smiling and arranges this colored cloth in front of me. I suppose I owe this kindness to the fact that I'm a foreigner."

The dice rolled again. Sokrat moved his piece forward.

"Everywhere you go, you've always been the object of

great solicitude, my dear. That's the way they catch frogs, with a simple scrap of scarlet rag. Don't misunderstand what I mean by my thought. It wasn't your vanity I was attacking, but your blindness. And this cloth on the table could just as well be a red pillowcase over your eyes."

I played and landed on the forty-second square.

"Should anyone land on forty-two, which contains a labyrinth, he will pay the stipulated price and return to square thirty," Sokrat recited, pleased with my bit of misfortune.

"A labyrinth, you say? Forest would be a more appropriate word."

"To get lost in a forest would certainly be an uncommon experience for someone in search of forgetfulness, Adam!"

"Sokrat, you shouldn't say 'get lost in a forest' but 'be lost there.' To be at the same time somewhere and nowhere. Inside a forest and outside of everything. To have lost one's direction: to be everywhere. Every branch, every bush, ditch, stump, piece of earth, fern, dead wood, moss, rut, path, pawprint or footprint, animal cry or bird song—everything is fixed. But nothing can be attached to that fixedness—no story, no character. Yet the things that are there aren't at all frightening. They are gentle and slow, in peaceful layers. Nothing moves in the forest if not the forest in place. Every tree is a mirror, every rock an echo. Everything that is smelled there, seen there, or heard there is already known and yet new. The first time is like the others: no two areas that resemble each other. They are all identical. No two forests alike. It's always the same. No space in a forest for someone who has gotten lost there. No string to get out and no pebble to drop from one's pockets. No shouts: a voice in a forest is only a sound the forest gives back to itself. The absence of space makes one dizzy; the lack of measure frightens. It's a stopped clock, a noiseless irregularity of direction, which has no beginning. For fear comes after, with the thought of a point of departure, in the idea of returning to the place where one got lost. To retrace one's steps: to feed one's fear. It's a very abstract circumstance; the forest causes the person who has gotten lost in it to walk. He goes round in a circle, believing he's finding the way out. To be driven crazy is the fate of the lost person. The forest has no other end but the trees he sees, no other edge but his inner rounds, no other center but his anxiety. Being neither a fox nor an owl, he remains forever alien to what is around him, alien to the forest, with no way out, but enclosed by nothing. For, unlike a labyrinth, a forest has no way out because it isn't closed anywhere. It is born suddenly of limitless fear."

A livelier gust of wind lifted an edge of the cloth and revealed a corner of the table, on which the waiter had just set down two more glasses of tea and some sugar.

"Adam," Sokrat said with an indulgent smile, "those are *the words of love*. It all comes from the fact that you don't know how to estimate distances correctly. It's a question of lenses, believe me, merely a question of lenses."

But perhaps an island, after all, was not such a poor observation post.

"I agree that it's a magnificent bridge, joining West to East as it does, above the Bosporus. And a daring idea! But don't expect me to go over it. That, I will not do."

"Adam," June insisted, "I would like it so much if you kissed me on the other side of that bridge. If you placed an Oriental kiss on my lips!"

No doubt whims are part of the charm of life. But I'm not whimsical and bridges make me uncomfortable.

"We'll take the boat," said Sokrat, smiling at June. "Adam won't be able to refuse us that. Besides, he knows very well that for a long time I've had something I wanted to show him over there. He knows it and he's afraid of it. But some day, my pal, some day when you're in a lighter mood, you'll explain to us what difference you see between this bridge and a boat."

I felt in a light mood and for me, in fact, there wasn't any difference between a bridge and a boat. I contented myself with answering June.

"An Oriental kiss, did you say? What a strange expression for 'a kiss in the Orient'!"

We had taken our places on a wooden bench on the upper deck. Thick smoke was billowing from the smokestack; under our feet we could feel the engine's vibrations in the planking. Sokrat was wearing a navy blue pea-jacket that made him look like a polar explorer in a comic book.

"It'll be cold if the wind blows from the Black Sea tonight, Adam."

June was lightly clothed, as usual. She claimed she had never been cold except for one Christmas night at Palmyra. Leaning her elbows on the handrail of the bulwark, her blond hair floating in front of her face and over her tanned shoulders, she turned three-quarters away from us and watched the crowd, thick at the approaches to the quay.

A strident, prolonged siren blast signalled the departure. After the mooring ropes were cast off and the propeller had begun slowly churning the soft waters of the Golden Horn, after the boat had entered the Bosporus, after Topkapi, in the distance, no longer resembled anything but a flattened gray barracks in the afternoon fog, June came back to join us on our bench.

"What does Adam think of our city?" Sokrat asked her, pretending to ignore my presence.

"That it's a dusty, noisy city," I observed aloud before June could answer Sokrat. "And smoky! Maybe you could explain to us how you manage to make so much smoke?"

"Adam's exaggerating, as usual," June remarked. "He actually loves being in Istanbul. He probably doesn't know it yet himself, but he'll agree later, once we've left. I imagine right now he's searching his tangle of memories for some possible resemblances with the new things surrounding him. Adam lives only through analogies."

"That's because he feels guilty, wherever he is, wherever he goes. I'm sometimes afraid his condition is getting worse."

"The worst thing, Sokrat, is that he doesn't change. Once—*this was a long time ago*—he came to join me in the summer on the island where I was spending my vacation. The whole time he stayed there, he felt miserable. At least he claimed he did. He showed no sign of contentment until the day he left. Yet I'm sure he now happily cultivates the memory of that visit so far in the past."

Leaving June and Sokrat to their conversation, I stood up and headed for the forward part of the boat, my camera in hand.

The island? Hanging from the clothesline under the vine of our blue courtyard, the two pieces of June's bathing suit were two white smudges in the darkness, at the level of my face. Standing in a corner of the courtyard, a cigarette in my hand, alone in this nocturnal scene, which wasn't yet familiar to me but was to become familiar, I gazed at the street entrance of our house, which had opened before me for the first time that same morning and which my blond lover, naked under her thin dress, had just closed behind her as she went out.

"What's going on, June?" I had murmured.

Half sitting up in bed, I felt my heart beating violently; my head was still echoing with the sudden din that had torn me from my deep sleep, from my first sleep in the peace of the island. I hadn't identified the noise that had startled me awake as this volley of furious hammering at the street entrance of our silent house in the middle of the night. But in the bright half-light, June lay on her back next to me with her eyes wide open and a calm expression on her face.

"For the love of heaven, why don't you answer me? What is going on?"

June had tossed aside the sheet, she had gotten up without haste, she had put on her yellow dress and, without any explanation, had gone out barefoot into the courtyard. Then I had heard the street entrance slam behind her; once again, in our room, the night was filled by the regular lapping of the water against the edge of the dock under the wide-open window.

My heart was not beating as hard. I went and sat down next to the well, on the other side of the small courtyard, and, following with my eyes the puffs of white smoke that emerged from my mouth and rose toward the starry sky through the leaves of the climbing vine, just now as black as its tight bunches of tart grapes, I waited for June to come back.

"What am I," I repeated to myself, finding a new formulation for an old question, "what am I doing here on this island?"

As my mute question dropped into the silence of the courtyard, the feeling of emptiness invading me only increased at the sight of the two pieces of the bathing suit, which, in the darkness, hung before my eyes like poisonous flowers.

"Don't waste your film, my friend! Soon there will be much better things for you, believe me!"

Sokrat was standing at my back while the boat moved away from the wooden pontoon bridge to make another, brief stop on the far bank of the Bosporus.

"Straight ahead of you, Adam! Open your eyes!"

As the sun went down, the evening of that first day on the island, as the lighthouse breakwater now sheltered us from Basile's raging threats, as June and I came back toward the port, our unused, dry beach towels rolled under our arms, walking along the quay where the water is deepest, where the names of the ships are painted on the stone in red in front of the mooring berths, my eyes fell upon a word carved at my feet and I stared at it in the oblique light—in the whole row, the only ship's name carved in the stone edge of the pavement.

Despite being worn down by the water and the soles of feet, the letters were still legible, the incised letters of the name Ate, daughter of Eris and Zeus, hateful to mortals and to the gods, Ate, evil goddess who speeds over the world sowing discord on earth and disturbance in people's minds.

Our dinner was silent. The wine was cool in the glasses. In the trembling light of the oil lamps, June's long hair shone on her bare shoulders. Her yellow dress suited the softness of her face, as her slow movements suited the curve of her chest. The darkness made her limpid eyes larger. And yet the noise of our silverware on the plates seemed to me sharper and sharper, louder and louder, in the summer night.

"And now, look at them, Adam! Look closely at these stone and air phantoms! Don't they remind you of anything?"

The engine roared under our feet. The water boiled for an instant under the reversed thrust of the propeller and the boat came broadside to the quay, which was hung with giant tires. It bounced once off the fenders while the men adjusted the moorings, and then was still.

Above our heads on the quay, stripped of its paving and invaded by grass, rose side by side the immense facades of two old palaces. Their windowpanes had been broken, and through the rows of naked openings one could see the sky under the still intact cornices where the collapsed roofs should have been. On the upper stories, the stone balustrades and the sculpted pediment bore black smoke marks. Because there was no gutter to collect it, the rainwater, streaming down, had produced wide whitish trails here and there along the marble colonnades. The steps of the broad flights of stairs which had once led down to the quay had in part disappeared and earth had filled in the spots where they used to stand. No one was bothering to look at these surprising relics.

Standing by the strait like monumental, abandoned stagesets, these ruined buildings nonetheless seemed to draw from the water that rocked their nonchalant reflections a simulacrum of an ephemeral survival, useless and happy.

"Well, Adam, what do you say to that?" Sokrat asked.

"That you flatter me, friend. Have you noticed how very different the reflections are from their source? Is it really possible that these heavy, pompous constructions find a moment of grace, at last, in the impalpable image of their downfall?"

"Now you're talking like a Byzantine florist trying to sell bouquets of faded flowers! But anyway, no one can maintain these Ottoman palaces any more. The one over there was struck by lightning recently and caught fire. They let it burn. It wasn't worth the water to save it. But from a distance, Adam, it still creates an illusion. And you'll see more of them before this evening."

"Now, I'd like you to visit my rock. We'll have to walk a little, but you'll see what an ideal place I've discovered for sunbathing and swimming where no one can see me. The water there is transparent; the light on the mountains intense by late afternoon."

June, already wearing her blue straw hat, rolled up the bath towels she had put out to dry under the vine in our courtyard, and while she laced up her leather sandals, I slipped on my white espadrilles, fully conscious of the solemn, intimate nature of this first visit to the island.

At the hour when the sun's heat lessened, the fig trees along the road behind our house were already exhaling a little of their evening smell—an ancient smell, harsh and bruised, that nestles in the depths of my intact olfactive memory. In the shade of the peaceful alleys that led to the port, life was slowly resuming its course after the daily siesta, the simple everyday life of a town or small island. The shopkeepers were reopening the doors of their stalls in a leisurely manner; the first customers, still drowsy, were making their taciturn appearances on the cafe terraces. In the water, amid the unmoving silence, empty boats bobbed over their mottled reflections.

Casual yet precise walkers, we rounded the port, passing in front of the closed post office, the customs building, and the harbor-master's office. After skirting the white tower of the lighthouse and leaving the jetty behind, we arrived at the site of the old boatyard. The ground was covered with a debris of wood and gray shavings on which the rust from the winches and the old anchors all in a line blazed in the light of the lowering sun, under the red oxide-painted hulls of a launch in dry dock and a boat under construction.

"We're almost halfway there," June said, slipping her hand into mine. "Don't you find that there's something frightening about this boatyard, Adam?"

"Navigation is a disquieting art, June, but on that gloomy art depends the life of an island. The shipwright and the knacker begin their work by felling trees and animals, in the red of birth, the red of the slaughterhouse and the shipyard."

As I was speaking these words, June's hand clenched in mine; the pressure of her fingers signaled me to stop walking.

"What's the matter, June?" I said, not understanding.

She had frozen, her lips pale, pressed together. Twenty yards or so in front of us on the dirt path, a short-legged man with feet far apart was gesturing and shouting.

"Let's not go any farther, Adam! There's no telling what he might do. Believe me, we should go back. I'll talk to him later, when he calms down."

Incredulous, I looked at the form that was blocking our way; even though it was impossible for me to make out the man's features since the light was behind him, I saw that he was highly agitated. When I heard my own name in the flood of abuse he was pouring out, his fist raised in our direction, I decided to take June's advice.

"What does he want?" I asked as we went back the way we had come.

"He and I spent last month together on his boat. He's the one who took me when I went to Rhodes to meet you."

As Sokrat had foreseen, the wind had risen on the Bosporus. To the north, the sky had clouded over; the waves were turning black and the current quickening. Our boat passed between the half-submerged wreck of a freighter and a row of tall wooden houses built at the water's edge.

Sokrat pointed out to me the gutted facade of one of them.

"It happened in broad daylight. There wasn't even any fog. The helmsman was drunk and went and drove the stem into an apartment on the second floor."

Off the port bow, a supertanker was heading back up toward the North Sea.

"When I saw him get off the plane in the middle of summer wearing his crumpled raincoat, I burst out laughing. You have to remember that in Rhodes and in the whole of the Dodecanese, it hadn't rained since March! And do you know what was in his suitcase, besides a few books and his toilet articles? His pillow! Did you know, Sokrat, that Adam never travels without carrying his pillow along with him in his luggage?"

"That," I observed, "is a secret that shouldn't have been given away. If you think of the time each of us spends sleeping in his life, you'll agree that we should be very particular about choosing a good pillow. And never afterwards be separated from it."

At Rhodes, that same evening, we had a grilled fish for dinner under the trees behind the ramparts. We were surrounded by patient cats; their eyes gleamed in the dark around our table whenever they turned their heads toward us. June was wearing her yellow dress; since we had last seen each other her skin had darkened in the sun.

Early the next morning, a taxi had taken us down deserted, flowery lanes to the port, where we had embarked for the island.

Once on board, disdaining the benches of the between-decks, we went straight to the forward part of the boat and—this was June's idea—climbed into a lifeboat. There we sat down amid a heap of ropes, canvases, and spars.

"The crossing lasts only a few hours," June said.

Soon, by the time Rhodes had disappeared from the horizon, the dazzling light of the sea in combination with the regular vibrations of the engines had caused us to be overcome by a sort of torpor close to sleep. But from this vessel, propitious because it was so slender, from the bottom of our sparkling lifeboat which smelled of brine and fresh paint, now and then breathing in a gust of warm air exhaled by an air shaft and blown back by the wind, I kept watch.

The deck of a boat is a geometrical white island, a floating form composed of iron, varnished wood, cables and glass, a perfect polygony of gleaming forces. This is not meant to be a brilliant allegory but the very approximate expression of an ordinary enigma. The *Panormitis* made the same crossing every day. It is quite likely that the sailors who made up its crew had long since become blind to what was around them, that their bodies and eyes had little by little been covered over with a second skin, scaly and opaque like the superimposed layers of paint on the rivetted plates and the watertight doors. But as June had said, for us the crossing would last only a few hours;

and a few hours is not enough time to be afflicted by that sort of blindness.

The shadow of the smokestack lay along the deck. When the ship heeled to one side, it swept through space like a dark projector and the light shifted onto other white surfaces, onto other windowed walls, overexposed and bleached like old daguerrotypes, while the spraying of the water under the bow accompanied, in a parallel, sonorous way, the regular swaying of the bulwark handrail in front of the horizon line.

"June," I murmured, leaning over her and stroking her hair, "what we lack is the vocabulary of navigation. What we know is useless to us here. We're only passengers. The vocabulary of navigation belongs to the ferryman."

Up above, on the bridge, behind the window of the wheelhouse, the motionless officer at the helm, a modern Charon in a uniform trimmed with braid, seemed like a waxen statue surveying the compass.

"He doesn't see anything, June, but he knows the password and we have merely paid for our passage. Tell me, did we keep the tickets? Did we in fact hold onto them?"

The sea was calm and the sky cloudless.

"This is a beautiful crossing, June. As beautiful as a dream."

June had fallen asleep. Lying between my legs, she had crossed over the distinct line of sleep; every last trace of sexual emotion had evaporated from her face. Her regular breathing lifted her breasts, bare under her half-open shirt. In the lifeboat, sparkling under the creaking blocks, her body, which transmitted to mine the ship's vibrations, now belonged wholly to the temporary, geometric, white world of our crossing.

"Adam," she asked me later when we were within

sight of the island, "does it ever seem conceivable to you that a woman might be a house?"

"A house, June? That may be true, actually. But not always. No, not always."

The door to the street entrance opened partway in the night. As the bright light from outside entered through the gap, June slipped into the small courtyard, closed the door behind her, and turned the key in the lock.

When she saw me there, sitting on the rim of the well, she came up, holding herself very erect in her pale dress, and stood there in front of me without moving.

Under my fingers, the rope of the bucket was coiled flat like a sleeping snake; above us, no breath of air moved the leaves of the vine.

June took my head in her cool hands and leaned her abdomen against my cheek.

"He's gone now," she said.

"The island? Sokrat, you could hardly imagine such consummate solitude! It's the most confined sort of place, the frozen simulacrum of a life preserved intact—not under a stream of lava or a rain of ashes, but in the color, the unchanging color. A pure theater of dispossession. Even the sound of the voices—the hideous speech of the island or the braying of the donkeys—doesn't fill a third of the distance separating the walls, the doors, and the tables. Such a great emptiness between things and such an implacable silence isolates more than a great uproar. Nothing grows on the island except wild sage, funereal trees, and prickly pear. It's a land without soil or water. Except for the black dresses worn by all the women and the white walls of the monasteries, everything there is embossed with color. Even the shadows. Everything there is within sight. That proximity limits traffic to the trajectories of habit and encloses each person in a locative existence that excludes fiction. For fiction, like everything that comes from outside, could only arrive by sea, with the shipments of merchandise, on the boats loaded with vegetables, with casks. Yet every part of the island turns its back on the sea. It's an abstraction petrified, truly discouraging to a lover of analogies."

Fortunately, there was June's rock. Fortunately, there was the possibility, on the island, of going back and forth between the house and June's rock.

The upper face of the rock was flat, with a gentle slope. Even though it was possible for the two of us to remain on the dazzling platform together, I had sat down a little ways back, on the crest of another rock; from my observation post, sheltered from the sun, I embraced with my gaze the transparent fan of morning landscape in the foreground of which June was lying on her stomach, her legs outstretched, her arms crossed under her head, which she had turned toward the sea. Her face was covered by her shining hair. On the bath towel spread out by her feet, her piled-up clothes formed a small filmy chaos of familiar materials next her watch and bottle of suntan lotion.

"No sight," I said to her, "awakens in me more good cheer than the sparkling of the morning light on the surface of a pale sea. Do you think this emotion comes from childhood or from the feeling diffused from a more distant source?"

"Adam," she answered in her cool, caressing voice, "I doubt you ever were a child. I'm not reproaching you for it, because I like you the way you are. But tell me, why do you refuse to expose yourself to the sun?"

"In a little while, June, in a little while, when we go in the water. Right now I'm busy struggling, as I do, stubbornly, every day, against the depressing invasion of blue. Have you noticed how strangely attracted the islanders are to this color? No matter which direction you look in, the sky and the sea invade three-quarters of the landscape. Why do the walls of the houses, the tables in the cafes, the iron curtains of the shops, most of them anyway, have to be painted blue? Even the boats—even the boats are blue!"

"Your eyes are blue, too, and it isn't unpleasant. Quite the contrary."

Behind her hip, near the spot where the small of her back formed a round hollow, the top of June's buttock bore a birthmark whose dark pigmentation contrasted with the light skin of her naked body. For a moment now, I had been staring at that dark spot, which was shaped like a butterfly wing and covered with a little down of short, silky hairs.

"Here," I had once declared to her, "is the incontestable mark of the ancient coat of hair, the sign that betrays the old savagery that each of us tries to shed, through a patient metamorphosis."

A gleam of distress had come into her eyes then, though it was immediately banished by the return of her confident smile. But after that day, the little velvety mark was never again the object of the least comment between us.

"June," I said, leaning over her from the top of my rock, letting my syllables drop down onto her tanned body, "your nudity deserves eulogies. It's a beautiful nudity. An exemplary nudity."

Was June smiling behind her screen of disheveled hair? I don't know, but I hope so. Nudity, like clothing, is a difficult art; and I have rarely seen anyone practice it with such convincing mastery. I don't think the obstacle is the greater or lesser beauty or harmony of the bodies, but the mistaken belief that, unlike clothing, nudity is a fact of nature. And that it is from the outset edifying. I read an account of an intimate meal among friends during which the guests exchanged pertinent and contradictory opinions on this subject. Yet I say nudity can't be the object of any discourse: too many divergent interests are aroused and intersect when it comes up. It's an unstable mirror.

I was admiring June's bare body lying on her white rock. I was marvelling over the mysterious work of the pearl which, around the little furry spot, had slowly modeled, year after year, the singular exactness, the radiant, tranquil assurance of her nudity.

"Yes, it's a beautiful mirror. But as far as I'm concerned, nudism relates to a completely different story. A story of very old rays of sunlight."

June reached for the pink towel. Before she could cover her body, the boat had appeared from behind the rocks

two or three yards away from us. Bundled in his faded
blue robe, the pope at the helm, rigid as a statue of poly-
chrome wood, was gazing straight ahead.

"He's going back to his monastery. He didn't see you,"
I said to June, who, her hands behind her back, was
hooking the bra of her bathing suit. She got to her feet
and stood for a moment on the edge of the rock. Then she
dove into the clear water, causing the cold foam to spurt
all the way up to my feet.

Later, when we were back in our little courtyard, when
June had hung up the two pieces of her damp bathing
suit to dry on the rope tied up in the shadow of the vine,
when I had drawn up from the well a pail full of fresh
water to wash down her salty body—she stood up on her
tiptoes, holding her breath, her eyes closed and her arms
lifted—the image of the arums rose in me with the light-
ning speed of a distress flare bursting in an empty sky:
the perfume of the arums, the lanceolate leaves and the
pale yellow pistils, dusted with pollen as white and soft
as talcum powder, at the centers of the trumpets. Yes, I
saw distinctly, under June's bare feet, the stone flights of
stairs that had once led down to the lower garden, the
steps clear and widely spaced.

"Quick, Adam! Hand me the towel. I'm cold."

June was scribbling some notes on a page of the notebook
in which she irregularly kept her journal. Sokrat was ab-
sorbed in reading a popular magazine. Without lifting his
head, he paused, frowning, to say that it hadn't rained

enough and the lack of water might be felt all summer.

"Lack of water, especially in summer, is a common problem," I answered politely.

Sokrat threw me an empty glance over the tops of his glasses and immediately plunged back into his suspicious examination of the magazine. Our boat was heading back down the Bosporus toward the Sea of Marmara. Long streaks of yellow were shredding the evening clouds.

"Adam," Aerea had said to me when we woke up the day I turned forty, "you're a good lover. This morning, we're going to take our bath together."

In the Manhattan bathroom, the water flowed over her smooth body; she kept her eyes closed because of the shampoo; the thin foam that slid over her gleaming curves made her look like an Anadyomene Aphrodite.

"My friend," said Sokrat, closing his magazine, "despite your predilection for ordinary spots, you shouldn't leave Istanbul without visiting Rustem Pasha's mosque."

The island's only industries are fishing for sponges and dressing them. The night before we left, June presented me with a sponge.

The air was brisk in the gangway. The white boat was passing close—a little too close, it seemed to me—to the island's outermost cliffs, which dropped precipitously into the sea. I had put my arm around June's waist and rested my hand on her hip.

"One more day and night of travelling," I said to her, "and we'll be free of the blue world of the islands!"

"Adam," she answered, "now that we're leaving, you suddenly seem happier. Won't you have any pleasant memories of the days we spent together on this island?"

"One day, on the rock, didn't you tell me you doubted I had ever had any childhood? Maybe it's not too late after all. I have to remain on my guard."

She leaned her head on my shoulder.

"Adam, I don't understand you. I was a happy little girl. I remember it perfectly. And I don't have the slightest doubt about it."

In my dream, the construction of the building was well advanced. Some forty storeys of glass and aluminum already rose beneath my feet into the clear sky of Manhattan. The quality of the reflections captured by those lofty walls of blue filled me with a legitimate pride.

Exacting architect inspecting his aerial worksite, I made the mistake, for a moment, of identifying with my work. I immediately felt metamorphosed into this mass under construction. Then things became more complicated: the materials intended for future storeys liquified and at that point it seemed to me obvious that the transmutation of glass and metal into water would compromise the continuation of the work. I experienced this liquid mass, glaucous, horizontal, as my own body, unfinished at chest height. Suddenly the last storey—even though its form, seen from outside, was that of a slab of water— turned into Aerea's body floating at the peak of the structure.

Guilty. But of what?

IV. GENERATION

All women, Adam? Without exception?"

Sokrat sits cross-legged on the edge of the carpet, his trunk upright, his head leaning slightly to one side. Sokrat sits facing my closed window; the reflections of the trees and sky in his thick glasses prevent me from seeing his eyes. In his right hand, he rotates his glass, and the noise of the little ice cubes knocking against the crystal is as sharp and clear as the tinkling of the signal bell in a bus. It is autumn again, the same autumn as always in front of my large window that looks out on the trees. It is once again the slow, the incessant silent motion of the leaves pierced through with twinklings that dance in the air and on the ground. My room is full of trees. I walk on a carpet of leaves. I'm not walking anymore. I'm an angel and angels have no feet. The ice cracks in my glass. In my glass, the bourbon is the color of the leaves. The sky is the very pale color of the pastilles that

61

dance in my memory, round, light, slightly acid, barely sweet, pastel blue, pastel yellow, pastel pink, pastel green. The pastilles fell on the carpet when the glazed paper twist came undone around them. I'm an angel. My blue wings are smooth and shiny. The sky tastes of scattered pastilles. My room is full of aromas and my glass is full of bourbon the color of the dead leaves that are falling beyond the window. I hear the blue rustling of the feathers on my back. Angels don't have their feet on the ground. Angels don't have feet. Sokrat looks like a Grand Vizier from a comic strip. The ancient Turks said that God created Adam first and placed him as a beautiful statue in Eden. The current is swift. As I wait for the bus, at the end of the bridge, I look at the water. I picked up a little gray leaf from the sidewalk on 53rd Street. In my tiny handwriting, I wrote *Columbus Day* in black ink on one face of the leaf. On the other, on either side of the midrib, I wrote our two names. But Adam's soul, which God had created separately, refused to come and animate the statue, pointing out that that perishable mass was not worthy of it. The bus moves alongside the river. The bus is full of reflections and flowers. God then sent his vizier Gabriel to play a tune on a flute near Adam's body. The bus is full of flowers; my glass is full of bourbon. At the sound of the archangel's instrument, the soul forgot its fears. It was touched and began dancing around the statue. In a drunken gesture, it entered Adam's body through the feet, which immediately began to move. My room is full of the reflections dancing in Sokrat's glasses. Aerea's blouse was of pale green silk. It was cold. The soul was ordered by God never again to leave its new dwelling. Since that day, the little gray leaf has blackened between the pages of a notebook, blackened so much that the two names written on either side of the midrib have become illegible. What remains is my memory of writing them. Perhaps memory is no more than a small surface that is becoming dark: one still knows what one will no longer be able to see. The little leaf is no more, now, than a black pastille dancing in my memory. My memory is a carpet growing dark, and Sokrat sits at the edge of my memory like a stubborn cormorant at the edge of a river, occupied with watching for fish in the water. The bus is full of flowers and the smells of flowers.

"Do you mean all women?"

What one will no longer see, like something far away, is a form of touch. The shadow of a tree on the grass at the end of summer. With a taste of geranium on the lips. The Vermont woods were flaming with the colors of October, as far as the eye could see under the sky. But autumn hadn't yet touched the leaves in Central Park. It was evening. Under the trees, it was already dark. The trees were green. The darkness falling from the branches mingled with the darkness rising from the ground. It was cold. The grass was drenched in the glacial, opaque, and maternal darkness in which my feet sank down, in which my feet disappeared from my sight while in my mouth the taste of geranium was warm and resonant. Above the trees the lower storeys of the buildings of Fifth Avenue were the color of ash. But up above, the upper storeys were bathed in their own light, soft, transparent, yellow, which seemed to pass through the stone, which seemed to come from it. The sky was blue above the terraces; the golden light played over the cornices and the domes of the water towers. There were trees on the terraces. Their little leaves shone in the silent air. In the cemetery, once upon a time, whitened stones sketched out rectangles where the graves lay. Flowers grew in the grass and on the graves. The air vibrated with the buzzing of the bees. Sokrat sits cross-legged on the end of a grave, in the midst of the flowers and the bees. The ice tinkles in his glass like a signal. Aerea was late. Before meeting me on 53rd Street, she had washed her hair. It was cold. On Fifth Avenue, the Columbus Day Parade had just ended. The sidewalks and the street were scattered with pastel pink, pastel yellow, pastel green, pastel blue confetti. We were walking along without speaking. Now and then the wind blew Aerea's fluffy hair over her eyes. She brushed it away with the back of her hand, laughing. Above our heads, the glass walls of the skyscrapers exchanged reflections in the brisk air. We were handsome. We were the same. Aerea put her hand in mine. She said she was hungry. To feed themselves, in the Garden of Eden, Adam and Eve breathed the perfume of the flowers and the fruits. Their translucent bodies were luminous. Inside the restaurant, it was hot. Our table was in front of a mirrored wall. Aerea had taken off her coat. On her green silk blouse, the mother-of-pearl buttons gleamed in the lamplight. Her eyes were shining. During lunch, we talked and laughed. Her lips were pale.

"Adam," she said in her melodious voice, "you're a fox. You're playing at seducing me."

Seduction isn't a game. Seduction, like alcohol, is a mirror in which, for a brief moment, death exchanges its mask for the mask of beauty. It's a natural inclination. Sokrat holds his glass in his right hand. Eve holds the fruit of the tree the way she would hold a little ice cube. Her gaze is lost in the infinite solitude and the distant dream reflected back to her by her own image or, identically, Adam's. Coiled up on the branch, the serpent, captivated, contemplates the sinuous nudity of the woman under the tree. It's the middle of the day. Behind the window, the yellow leaves make no noise. He contemplates his glass. I turned my eyes away from Aerea's face. My eyes rested on her image in the mirror. The restaurant was filled with the buzzing of the bees. Aerea's beauty was even more imperious, more resplendent, in the mirror. The leaves fall behind the window. The leaves fall into the river. The bus was filled with the reflections of the sun in the windows. Aerea's hair smelled good. As we left Central Park, she requested a stop by ringing the signal bell. In a drugstore on Columbus Avenue she bought some lipstick. She put some on her lips and asked me if it suited her. I walked her back to the front of her house.

"Adam," she said, taking her keys out of her purse, "you'd better leave me now."

On the first step of the stairs, there were many bundles of old newspapers tied up with string. I kissed Aerea. Her lipstick tasted of geraniums. In Central Park, the trees were green. The light of the setting sun lit the tops of the buildings along Fifth Avenue. There were no clouds. On the other side of the portholes, the sky was becoming light in the east. Now it was night in Central Park. The hostess brought the plates containing our breakfast. Her perfume smelled of heliotrope. The cabin was full of the buzzing of the bees. Sokrat sighed. Sokrat had a habit of punctuating his questions with a sigh. Sokrat's questions dropped like sighs or smiles.

"Flowers, Sokrat, yes. All of them without exception."

V. HALOES AND GLORIES

Every night, I'm kept awake by insomnia. For hours, in the dark, the tapestry of my days unravels: images and thoughts gradually lose their contours. Then I feel my mind and body crumble. In my dusty fits of insomnia, I sometimes even have the sensation that I am no more than a pinch of dry powder between the sheets and could be entirely contained in the ashtray of frosted glass on my table.

When the two sash windows capture the first glimmers of dawn, when the birds begin cheeping in the trees around the Museum of Natural History, when the apartment's radiators begin whistling, I go back to sleep. Then I dream. And in my dreams, Aerea leaves me again.

"It's a live present," June said, putting the brown paper bag down in front of me.

Through the wide open windows, the noise and light of Columbus Avenue invaded the room. The morning was sunny and the temperature was mild for the end of December. Among the leafless trees, the massive pink stone of the Museum of Natural History blocked the view of Central Park. I cautiously drew the little Savanna Cypress out of the brown paper bag and set it on a rectangular plate covered with a layer of damp gravel.

"Adam, this tree is nine years old. It can live two hundred years and remain the same size. But without the proper care, it can also die in four days."

June's voice was calm, caressing. In its dark earthenware pot, my dwarf cypress spread its green leaves an inch or two above the clump of mossy earth in which its roots were imprisoned.

The pears were small. They tasted of wax. But they were delicately swollen, smooth and soft to the touch. I gathered them one by one among the irises. Perched in the pear tree, Médé made them fall at my feet by shaking the branches.

I liked to hold them in my small hands, just as I liked

their green, red, and yellow colors. I was aware, though still a little confusedly, of the kindness shown me by the old man dressed in his white jellaba; it was for me that he had climbed up into his fruit tree.

"Adam," said Aerea in surprise, "I don't understand your aversion to fruit."

"My friend," Sokrat said to me as we were crossing the Galata bridge toward the Egyptian Bazaar, "instead of a heart and a soul, you have three sections of mirror. It seems that a true soul has never vibrated in you. Do you even have a life of your own?"

Today, I miss his deep, harsh voice, as I also miss his sharp, kindly reflections.

Why did I come back? Why to this particular apartment, situated behind the Museum of Natural History, above the peaceful restaurant where we so often came to have dinner by candlelight, Aerea and I, surrounded by mirrors and climbing plants? Why did I break the silence that was beginning to fall once again over the forests of Manhattan?

"I wouldn't have thought you were capable of running so easily."

A touch of admiration could be heard behind the irony in Aerea's voice. We had just finished running around the Reservoir a third time and had thrown ourselves, breathless, onto a grassy slope. The noise of the traffic on Central Park West came to us through the branches; beyond the latticework of the tall chain link fence, the evening breeze erased all reflections from the surface of the water. I have always been a good runner: even though my wind is beginning to go, my heart still beats slowly.

At the foot of the aromatic eucalyptus, the stone steps rose in tiers through the curved, silent space of the stadium, empty at sunset. After a first lap around the track, gradually accelerating my pace, my light feet rebounding from the fine pink gravel, my entire body having become a perfect mechanism, a gyrating top set spinning upon the rim of a crystal bowl, capable of turning a very long time without fatigue, drawing the energy it needed from its uniform movement, I watched as though from a distance, with the calm, proud detachment of an experienced mechanic, the slightest vibration of my young organs, the regular panting of my respiration, and I would run like this in the deserted stadium until a delicate fog composed of thousands of points of light formed before my eyes and my veins tingled delicately, warning me of imminent danger. Then I would end my evening race and remain motionless for a long time, supremely alone, standing at the edge of the grass listening to the blood beat under my skin.

Lying on her back in the grass in Central Park, her eyes half closed and her mouth open, Aerea slowly caught her breath. While I looked at her, I wondered if, when he left the stadium after his daily race, as the darkness invaded it, the child I was then had any inkling that he would later become a good lover because his heart beat so slowly.

At nightfall, the hundreds of fragile incandescent mantles of the acetylene lamps hanging over the market stalls transformed the Square of the Great Sokko into a blinding, teeming mass in which the light was so white and so harsh that it reduced almost to silence the din of voices and shouts that mingled with the nocturnal sounds of the drums and little nasal flutes.

"This is our Christmas celebration," Médé had explained, leaning on me.

In the dazzling, cold light of the lamps, his beard was as white as his turban.

"With you, Médé, I'll never be afraid," I had answered, lifting my eyes to him.

With one hand, I gripped very tightly the hand of the old mountain warrior turned gardener, basket weaver, and house caretaker; with the other, I held against my chest the cone of newspaper into which Médé piled colorful candies and dried fruits as we made our way through the turbulent darkness of the crowd. I clasped in my hand the cornucopia in which the old man deposited at last, topping it off, a little blue ceramic drum. When the smell of charcoal fires came to me in gusts, I nearly fainted with happiness.

Once we were over the Galata bridge, Sokrat led me into the Egyptian Bazaar.

"And yet you're alive! You even have quite a full life for someone so empty!"

In the center of the Bazaar, in the incessant disorder of colors, voices, and smells, the little mosque lifts up its blue order and its silence. Inside the sanctuary, the wall covering sparkles, in the shadowy light, with all the various blues of Ismir. The arabesques and the lineaments of the decor are organized into a living disorder similar to the disorder of the waves in the sea or the leaves in a forest. Among the sheens of the silk carpets, the leaded glass windows and the multicolored chandeliers, the sheens of the walls of faience and the pillars ringed with copper, two times intersect the way waters mingle in the Bosporus: the blue time of Ismir, of Fatima, daughter of Suliman, and the present time of the Bazaar, frozen by the black needles on the faces of the English watches. Two times are exchanged in silence; in this crossed time, two silences mingle in a larger silence. The petrified silence of history and of names; the silence of the spirit to which aspire the peace-seekers. In the luminous rustling of the mingled silences and times of the little mosque of

Fatima, two mosques are noiselessly superimposed: the austere mosque of Suliman, which commands the Golden Horn, and the great blue mosque of Mohammed, which gazes out at the Sea of Marmara.

The princess's wish was that her mosque should be fully equal, in its magnificence, to the other mosques of Istanbul. But the sum of money she managed to gather did not allow for building more than a mosque of modest dimensions. A construction of small size would have gone unnoticed among the jumble of other constructions in the Bazaar. What was more, the site chosen exposed it to the danger of floods. The architect solved the difficulties this way: so that the future mosque would be quite visible to the eyes of everyone despite its small size, he had the idea of raising it by one storey. In so doing, he protected it from floods. And in the basement of the building, which is on the same level as the rest of the Bazaar, he had the idea of installing shops whose rent would defray, in times to come, the costs of maintaining the sanctuary. Fatima approved of these plans. She had the sparkling volume of bluish light raised above the money and the floods. In the middle of the Bazaar, above the noises and the voices of her century, she established the silence of her blue ceramic garden. Among the shimmering, peaceful reflections of the air and the stone, she raised her heart's prayer above her time.

Sokrat took photographs of the interior of the mosque.

"For you, my friend! For you!"

Then he led me into the courtyard and pointed to the wall of the peristyle.

"Look at this carefully. Because the Garden of Eden bore within it its own limits, every building conceived in its image has to show its limits also. So that the visitor's soul may not remain captive of this place, a defect breaks its harmony."

As he is on the point of passing through the entryway, no one can fail to be surprised by what will appear to him at first a clumsy, hasty restoration of this part of the decor. The geometrical arrangement of the arabesques and the blue and red tracery is upset: muddled lines and colors, drab hues of wilted flowers.

The speed of the wind and the clouds in the blue sky. Glinting crests of the little waves. Walking along the Hudson, at Christmas, in Riverside Park, walking through the dead leaves that had fallen that autumn. The noise and brightness of the leaves on the ground. I listened to them, I listened to them crackle under the soles of my shoes. Their curled edges gleamed in the sun. Shadows and glimmers of light. Brilliant and dull surfaces. Suddenly, a little jumble of leaves rumpled under my steps. In all that crisp expanse, the little eddy of leaves like any others. Suddenly there. But nothing special. Nothing but a brief dizziness of light and leaves. The noise they made. Scarcely the scurrying off of a lizard. Black snag in the day. Then, suddenly, the smell of other leaves—*it was a long time ago*—in the dead leaves of Riverside Park, glimpsed in a lightning quick flash, beyond my grasp under my feet in the chaos of dead leaves. Empty recollection; which can't be tied to anything.

Afterwards, there was the squirrel. Afterwards, there was once again the expanse of dead leaves on the ground, the lapping of the water, the fast-moving clouds above the Hudson, the wind. There was once again the blue sky and the noon light reflected back by the heavily-ornamented facades of the buildings that lined the river.

A few feet away from me under a tree, a motionless squirrel, alert, was watching me with its round eyes. Aerea never managed to pronounce the French word for "squirrel," *écureuil*. Every time she tried, she would push out her lips as though for a kiss, but no sound would come out of her mouth.

"Don't ever forget this little catastrophe of painted ceramic, Adam," Sokrat went on. "This is the snag in the net, the rent through which anyone who knows how to remain vigilant can escape from the blue quietude and the drowsiness of the spirit, the way a fish slips out of the net in which it has let itself be caught and was swimming round and round."

What is needed is a wretched garland of green, blue, and yellow lightbulbs illuminated during the night of December 24 around the windows of a corner building on Columbus Avenue, for Manhattan to appear to me once again like a dead city. All that is needed is this naive decoration—a few bare lightbulbs hanging from a wire during the night before Christmas—for the facades of Manhattan to become, once again, in my eyes, the great inanimate backdrop before which Aerea and I had exchanged our first remarks and our first smiles.

When Médé died, I remembered the grasshoppers that we had grilled and eaten in silence, he an old man and I a child, the two of us squatting side by side in a corner of the ravaged garden. After the swarm of grasshoppers had passed, nothing was left of his plantings. All that remained on the stripped earth were a few stupefied grasshoppers and a little circle of lentils in leaf which I had sown myself and which Médé had protected in time with an overturned basket.

When he died, it was this little circle of green lentils that I thought of.

On the eve of Columbus Day, the Wall Street district was deserted under the rainy sky; light was rare in the narrow, sunken streets. Here and there, through holes in the pavement, small jets of white steam rose whistling.

"So, Aerea, here we are alone at the heart of the world!"

"Adam," she answered, "no one ever comes here at the weekend. There's nothing to do here, nothing to see."

In the air of Manhattan, old skyscrapers that borrowed their architecture from all times and places bulked high above our heads, rising in stages. Behind the rows of identical windows, no light shone. In the middle of the autumn afternoon, the silence was as deep as in a timber forest at nightfall. Aerea was silent too. Under her fur jacket, she was wearing the blue pullover I had seen on her the day we met: she was coming back from the Metropolitan Museum. She had brought back from it a postcard reproduction of a Persian miniature portraying a hunt. A detail of the painting showed a stag mating with a doe.

"You're right," I said to her. "The heart of the world is a very old mirror. There's nothing more to see here."

On December 24, in the late afternoon, two bums occupied a bench on Columbus Avenue. The first was seated, and held in his hand a flask of liquor, half full. The second was standing, one foot on the sidewalk and the other on the bench. He was threatening his companion with the filed blade of a penknife.

"Say that again, and I'll kill you!"

The other muttered a curse and held the flask out to his aggressor, who gently pushed it away.

"Say that one more time, and I'll kill you!"

And once again, he patiently pushed away the flask that the other, swearing, held out to him.

In the midst of the general indifference of the people walking by, two actors were playing the scene of universal repetition.

Darkness came abruptly in the middle of the day, and in the tumult of clouds and the glare of the first bolts of lightning, the waters of the sky swept down on the city.

The rain, falling in buckets on the sidewalks and rushing down the pavements, emptied the streets of their pedestrians and paralyzed all traffic.

I was caught in it on Central Park West. Soaked from head to toe in less than a minute, I went on walking. Around me, an imperious silence, which one could only divine behind the water's din, had invaded the deserted city. One recognizes such a silence by the difference it makes in one's perception of space.

Have you had the experience, reader, of living for some time with wax in your ears? Starting from the second day, the diminution of the familiar noises that punctuate the hours of your days and nights gives you the impression of moving and thinking in a strange environment. Sounds no longer form a boundary for your gestures as they did before. Smells and tastes change. Colors have a different luster. When you read or write, you find that your sense of the language and time has been modified: you no longer hear the sound of the pages that you turn. However infinitesimal it may be, a change takes place in your way of seeing and understanding what is around you.

Behind the curtain of rain, this imperceptible, profound silence had split the city in two. Above the city drowned under the deluge, a second, celestial city, as though disengaged from its foundations, was pushing up toward the torn sky its spectral shapes, striated again and again by the vertical strokes of lightning.

To the lively beat of a drum, the students in the class were executing precise figures under the direction of the dance teacher, a rather small black man, elderly but surprisingly agile. The mirror that covered the entire length of the main wall of the dance studio reflected the mobile and colorful image of the ballet. In the wall opposite the mirror, the windowpanes were veiled in violet glimmers every time a bolt of lightning traversed the darkness outside. The room was brilliantly lit and its parquet floor gleamed. The drum covered the noise of the rain and the thunder.

Her hair gathered and knotted in a ribbon, Aerea, in a green leotard, was moving about among the other dancers. When she saw me, all dripping with rain, standing in the doorway, I knew from her smile that I had been right to come and that she would be happy to dance before my eyes. She could count on the support of my gaze, which would follow every motion she made.

Suddenly a handful of plaster broke off from the ceiling and fell on the waxed parquet. The dancers froze and the teacher walked up to the little heap of white powder and studied it for a moment without saying anything.

He asked for someone to bring him a scoop and a whisk broom. With meticulous gestures, he collected the plaster dust in a paper envelope and wiped the remaining traces from the floor with a rag. After which, the dance started up again to the lively beat of the drum.

Later, when Aerea had changed and joined me, as we were about to leave, the small man passed by close to us, his drum in his hand. Aerea spoke to him.

The smile he gave her, which included me, reminded me of the smile Médé used to reserve for me.

Around and above us, Wall Street was isolated in its own silence. Through the play of reflections, the heart of Manhattan sank deep into its false memory: reflections of skyscrapers in the puddles; reflections of the facades of buildings in the facades of other buildings. The most recent constructions, all with blue or black glass walls, redoubled by their mirror effects the images of the old buildings lifting to the sky their jumble of petrified dreams: Venetian palaces, Gothic cathedrals, kiosks and minarets, pagodas, ziggurats, ruined terraces invaded by wind-sown grass. The strange and distant nostalgias that haunted their builders had thus marked the city.

"Imagine the day when the old stone skyscrapers will all have been replaced by glass towers, giant mirrors reflecting back at one another only the empty images of other giant mirrors. At that point, Aerea, the city will have completed the cycle of its history and when you look up, you will see only the blinding reflections of light on glass. Have you thought about this?"

"What we need most," my old friend Montalban said to me, "is a lot of patience."

As he talked to me in a voice roughened by tobacco and alcohol, he mopped his forehead with a white handkerchief. In the furnace-hot wooden shack, in the midst of an inextricable tangle of broken pottery and shards of faded frescoes, oil lamps, fragments of statues and sculpted stones, lachrymatories and glass phials, cups full of coins coated with verdigris bearing worn effigies, he showed me a large earthen vase, round and glazed, with no decoration but the random figures formed by the plaster in the spots where there were pieces missing.

"For months, now, I have been looking for the pieces to this vase and putting them together. I'm quite confident I'll find them all and be able to finish this work some day. But for that, we'll need a lot of patience, a lot more still."

Why did my lamented friend say *we* in speaking of those splinters of his fragmented life? Why?

Reader, have you ever seen a jellyfish moving along under the water? Have you admired its unfurled umbrella and the undulations of its iridescent filaments? Doesn't it seem to be gently letting itself be borne along by an invisible underseas current? And have you noticed how eagerly the minuscule fish that escort it surround its diaphanous form?

Sitting on a public bench on Broadway, I breathed the sea air that had been driven by the wind into the center of the island. To the north, on the avenue, the windows of the buildings surmounted by their watertowers reflected a sky as green as pools at low tide. Around me now, at sunset, the flood of people walking by swelled and then subsided, their voices and languages passed through me as though I were made of glass.

Night had fallen during dinner, a warm, early July night in New York. I was placed not far from the windows, to the right of Aerea, who was talking to a movie actress. On the table, now cleared, the flames of the candles cast their unsteady gleams over the glasses and rumpled napkins. The disorder of a table after a meal is like the disorder of a bed in the morning.

I was scarcely giving more than half my attention, by now, to the remarks being exchanged. Behind my dark glasses, I felt myself slowly drifting through the laughter and conversation of our hosts and the other guests. Amid the din of words Aerea's voice reached me now and then. We had first met in this same room, the eve of Columbus Day.

In an apartment in the building opposite, on the other side of Lexington Avenue, men and women were standing, glasses in their hands, before a refreshment table placed against the wall. Suddenly, they all put their glasses down and began psalmodizing. The siren of a police car drowned out for a moment the scraps of their song that came to me through the open windows. Then they danced a farandole: while still continuing to sing, they went round and round in the bright apartment, holding one another by the hand. A little of their joy warmed me from a distance. I was cold. The dance and the songs stopped as abruptly as they had begun. Everyone left. When the apartment was entirely empty, the lights were turned off.

"You didn't say a word to me all evening," Aerea reproached me as we were walking, half an hour later, toward Fifth Avenue, looking for a taxi.

I had nothing to say in answer to her. Aerea stopped on the edge of the sidewalk, put her arms around my neck, and gave me a long kiss. A moment later, she pushed me away with the utmost coldness.

Back in the small apartment, she came and sat down next to me opposite the fireplace, where the brass cusps of the andirons gleamed among the ferns. She crept into my arms and began crying.

Later, she fell asleep on the large purple carpet, wrapped in the white sheet.

I am alone in a garden, on the morning of December 25. In the middle of winter, the garden is in flower: everywhere around me, spring colors glow. I stand in the middle of the garden, in the center of a patch of earth that is black and very dry, without vegetation.

In my Christmas dream, I pour water on the sleeping earth.

But I will never have a chance to tell this dream to Aerea.

VI. VIRGINIE

At the beginning of the dream, I am writing. I have the impression that it is night. Yet no lamp is lit on board and through the opening that gives access to the deck, I see that the sky is light. Have I slept in my dream? The almost imperceptible rolling, the metallic clinking of a halyard striking the mast at regular intervals, the gentle lapping of the water against the hull tell me that the boat is not moving. Opposite me, on the other side of the mahogany table, leaning back against a partition of smoked plexiglass that separates her bunk from the card table, my very young wife, Virginie, is immersed in reading a book. With her right hand, she is tolding her blond hair up off the nape of her neck. The light falls through the porthole onto her shoulders and bare breasts. In my dream, marriage has turned me into a level-headed man, henceforth capable of more than merely strong but transitory emotions. I have undertaken a long and exacting task whose progress I note down scrupulously every day in the notebook that is open before me on the table. Even though the exact nature of this work is still not well known to me, I know that my presence on board is directly related to it. I am confident in the future. At this point I reread the lines I have just written on one page of the notebook. The more often I reread them, the more confused their meaning becomes, escaping me. Her loins wedged in among the cushions, Virginie has leaned her elbows on the bunk. Her nude hip is resting against the edge of the varnished table. The tips of her tanned breasts have hardened and on her flat abdomen the lower edge of her bathingsuit forms a bright blue trapezoid that swells up slightly. Now and then she looks up at me with loving tenderness. In my dream, Sokrat, whose presence I hadn't noticed before, is sitting at the card table. His eyes lost behind his thick glasses, his chin resting in the palms of his hands, he seems preoccupied, almost menacing. Not a word passes among us and the silence in the place is disturbed only by Virginie's sighs. Why has my young wife started sighing? The light has changed. The boat has turned on its anchor. I see Virginie absorbed in reading her book, her eyes lowered, her slender legs folded up under her. Now her expression is grave and distant. At the sight of her beauty, so fragile, I am overcome by great emotion, but I don't dare speak to her. I tear a page out of the notebook lying in front of me, write on it that I love her, and slide it across the table separating me from her and in among the open pages of her book. Now her body loses a little of its sheen. "That's the effect," I say to myself with regret, "that words have on bodies in love—to make them opaque." The sun is going down. The wind has fallen. Her face closed, Virginie stands up and leaves the cabin. The brief look she gives me in passing is cold. She busies herself on the deck. I admire her suppleness, her precise, graceful movements. She seems sure of herself. Even in the midst of exertion, the delicate frame of her body seems to be at rest. The boat is anchored in the middle of a bay. Her silhouette bowed before the clouds, Virginie stands with one hand on a shroud. Her eyes are full of tears. Sokrat mentions to me a yellow lath belonging to Virginie that has probably fallen into the sea. What he's talking about is a rigid blade of some plastic material about a foot and a half long. "The waves," he says, "will have taken it up onto the beach." I swim around the boat. On one side of the hull, it is day, on the other side, night. As I pass back to the day side, Virginie, laughing, pours wine into my mouth from up on the deck. The wine is lukewarm and it tastes familiar to me. I swim toward the beach. I can't see the bottom, even though the water is transparent. The arc-shaped bay is oriented in a north-south direction. At low tide, a line of sand separates its beach from a lagoon. Having come up on the land at the center of the bay, I explore first the northern part of the shore, looking for Virginie's lath. As I am retracing my steps without having found it, I think I see it suddenly in the shallow waters of the lagoon. But the object I retrieve and hold for an instant in my hand is only a piece of a soft, yellow strap that was probably the handle of a bottle of detergent. The sun has set. My progress becomes difficult: to the south, the beach narrows. Violet flowers grow in the sand less than a yard from the water. I have lost hope of finding Virginie's lath. Now it is pointless for me to go on: my search no longer has any object. My bare feet sink deeper into the wet sand. I have the feeling, confused at first, then completely clear, that I am placing each of my steps in a moment that I have already experienced. Not that I am going back over the course of my past life, but that I am finishing what remained unfinished in it. I understand that for me there exists neither before nor after; what I took for my memories were only warnings of what is happening now. "That," I say to myself, "is a revelation that deserves to be set down in my notebook." But the notebook is back on the boat. Now I'm in a hurry to reach the far end of the beach. There, I'm sure, I will find the beginning and the end of my efforts. Then I will be able to explain to Sokrat that my entire life has been contained in a single day, under the arc described by the sun between one morning and one evening; that each new day will have been only a recurrence of a single day fractured by the kaleidoscope of the seasons and the years; and that, finally, my life is contained in the space of this bay, a white rainbow in which recollections and premonitions are strictly reversible luminous signals. Yes, Sokrat would be happy to hear me tell him all that. And Virginie? At the end of my dream, my heart beats deeply inside the sand. The boat is still motionless in the middle of the bay. There is no one on board.

VII. COLOR, THEN . . .

Situated about seventy nautical miles off the Sahara, Cecilia is the northernmost island in the archipelago. The island next to it, from which it is separated by an elongated strait known as the Rio, looms up over it with a gray cliff against which the clouds come colliding in the late afternoon when the northern wind, the region's dominant wind, is blowing.

Opposite this cliff, on Cecilia's south coast and by the Rio, lie the port and the pueblo where the fishermen's families live throughout the year, comprising the island's entire population. Immediately beyond the first houses begins a desert expanse of sands and lava fields. There is no water on Cecilia except for that produced for the needs of daily life by the small seawater desalinization plant, a building of glass and white clay that sparkles in the sun between the first dunes.

"Our girls," says Remedios, turning her glass of gin

fizz in her hand, "are much too hot-blooded for our phlegmatic boys. I've surprised more than one lurking in the dark at a bend in a lane, waiting for the bars to close so they can lure away some *green fly* walking back to his quarters outside our village. They have the souls of sirens."

What we see is the exact replica of what we know. I have seen glimmering, at night, at the foot of the dunes, the unbuckled belts of the soldiers to whom these precocious young girls give themselves with emphatic moans of pleasure. In the darkness, their hair has the sheen of fishscales and their bodies bared on the sand are as pale as the white bellies of fish. When the moulting is finished, the red crabs leave behind on the rocks their empty carapaces, light envelopes, perfectly formed, that shatter at the mere pressure of one's fingers. At the hour when the sun goes down, the boats go back out onto the Rio to fish for iridescent squid, while on the sloping square, in front of Don Miguel's cafe, at the junction of the jetty and the beach on which purple nets are drying, the women clean fish for dinner. Ichthyophagous dogs observe them from a distance out of their slow, faded eyes. When night has fallen, the soldiers whom Remedios nicknames the *green flies* make their entrance, in little groups, into the gloomily lit cafes where they come to vie with one another in their noisy games of dominoes, interrupted, around midnight, by the extinguishing of the lights: the engine of the freshwater and electricity plant dies and the entire island is abruptly plunged in darkness. Until the next morning, the pueblo is invaded by the silence of the sands.

Yes, what we see is an endless mirror. But what do we know of the rent that is caused in us when our gaze meets another? I'm also talking about the gaze of the fish I catch and the gaze of the old volcanoes, which are slowly petrifying us. Remedios knows these things well: her eyes have the power to soothe such wounds. After the *Green House* closes, I often find her sitting on the front steps, where she waits for me smoking her mentholated cigarettes. In the sandy lanes my rope-soled espadrilles make no noise. The dreaming dogs recognize me and let me pass without even raising their heads.

The day I arrived, I refused the room with the view of the Rio that Don Miguel had prepared for me. My window looks out, when the sun comes up, on the dunes and the volcanoes. In the morning, I am awoken by the plant's engine resuming its throb in the silence. At that hour, the streets are deserted. The sea is flat and gray. The curved cones of the volcanoes haven't yet taken on any definite color. Laundry that has been drying since the day before on a rope strung between two white walls is the only apparent sign that there is life inside the houses.

The nights on Cecilia are not enough to mend the fatigue of the days. They mark only brief pauses in the irreversible exhaustion that is slowly consuming this world cut off from the world, of which it presents scarcely more than a weakened and distant echo. A few days are enough for me, as an outsider, to study most of the words used in daily life. The island is totally without relics of the past. Storms and tides do not bring flotsam up onto its coasts, not even the usual plastic refuse that the ocean in all latitudes throws up onto beaches where the sun gradually discolors them. Cecilia has no history apart from the long degeneration of its inhabitants.

"By continuing to intermarry," Remedios says to me, "they will end up making this island the main reservoir of idiots in the entire Atlantic Ocean."

I have come out noiselessly to study the sky and the sea from the end of the jetty. Remedios is the last clear form in this declining world, to which she nevertheless belongs body and soul.

Juan waits for me every morning behind his mother's bakery, listening to the radio sitting behind the wheel of the only motorized vehicle on the island, Don Miguel's Land Rover. With feigned alacrity, he helps me load the back seats with the rods and lines and the canvas shopping bag containing my lunch and the bucket of fresh sardines I use as bait.

I get into the front seat next to Juan and tell him which spot I've chosen to fish from that day. The shake of his head is more eloquent than a disapproving remark.

Once past the desalinization plant, the Land Rover bumps along one of the tracks that cross Cecilia, skirting the volcanoes. In sand bristling with stones and lapilli, we are shaken about as though in a small boat, "because," Juan claims with a smile, "the relief on land is identical to the relief under the sea." I suspect, in fact, that he takes the same pleasure in accentuating the jolting of the vehicle as in making the bracelet-watch he wears on his wrist glitter in the sun. But I merely cling to the door without paying any attention to his mocking half-smile. When we reach our destination, he stops the Land Rover at the edge of a scree overlooking the ocean.

"Juan," I say, unloading my fishing gear, "when you come back to get me this evening, honk to let me know you're here."

As I descend among the black rocks with my load, I hear him driving off through the dunes. He is returning to the village where he will busy himself, in the back room of the bakery, with all sorts of minor illicit activities such as the clandestine filling of air bottles for the underwater fishermen who come from the neighboring islands to poach in Cecilia's waters.

Once I reach the wave-battered lava platform, I patiently rig my lines: I spend my days with the fish.

Standing behind the polished wood bar, Rosita set out glasses and bottles of beer on a tray and then carried it to the far end of the room. Sitting at our table, Don Miguel followed her with his eyes for a moment. Then he took off his delicate glasses, cleaned the lenses, and examined them in the light from the electric lightbulbs before answering the question Remedios had asked him. When he smiled, his thin lips revealed two rows of small, crowded teeth, but his words were lost to me in the general din of the cafe, among the sharp clatter of the dominoes on the tables and the exclamations of the players.

"Don Miguel," Remedios explained to me, "hopes his daughter will go on helping him run the cafe and the hotel. but he knows Rosita has other ideas. She has eye-brows shaped like paddles. At the first opportunity she will leave Cecilia. And it won't be Juan who will keep her here. No, he won't be the one to stop her from leaving!''

A tall young man entered the cafe. His skull, com-pletely bald, shone under the ceiling light. The soldiers greeted him as he went by. He headed straight toward us, absentmindedly shook the hand Don Miguel held out to him, and sat down across from me in a chair to the left of Remedios.

"Adam," she said, introducing the newcomer, "Don Sebastian is my protector. He's also veterinarian to these *green flies* buzzing around us. Here, the fact that he's the army medical officer earns him deferential treatment from everyone; but you don't have to show him the same re-spect."

Don Sebastian smiled at me, asked after my accommo-dations, and immediately talked to me about fishing. When his duties left him some free time, he himself went in for underwater fishing, "but without bottles," he said. He was convinced that Cecilia's immediate future was threatened by three curses. First, the underwater divers who went down and hunted the fish into their lairs, where they massacred them point blank, obliging the sur-vivors to seek refuge in waters ever shallower and farther away; second, those inexperienced in laying nets or the victims of the maliciousness of other inexperienced poachers: should a storm or a severed anchoring rope prevent them from bringing their nets back up in time, the imprisoned fish die, and their rotting flesh infests the water, causing the other fish to flee it forever; third, those who tend, at the entrance of the narrows or across the feeding currents, their accursed *three-mesh* nets, which are gradually emptying the sea of its inhabitants.

In every place where there is any animation at all, the general noise of voices yields, now and then, to unpredictable beaches of silence: all conversations stop at the same time, to resume immediately all the more vigorously. Is this alternation random or does it obey the same secret laws as the roaring of the waves and the wind? I don't know. It was during one of these lulls that Juan pushed open the door of the cafe. At first he stood still on the threshold, gazing around with a bold look—even though no one had paid any attention to him—at the people who were there. Then, crossing the smoky room, he headed straight for the far end of the bar, behind which Rosita greeted him with a nice smile.

The brief silence that had coincided with Juan's arrival had also put an end to our conversation about fishing. In the hesitation that followed (reminding me of the strange calm that precedes the turning of the tide, a truce during which the ocean stops *pulling* on its waters and the fish no longer bite), Remedios pivoted on her chair and leaned toward me. Her glance met mine. Almost at the same time, she smiled at me.

This smile (with which she looked me down and up instead of up and down, as would have been suitable for a such a smile) was not, in fact, marked by the blissful gravity the old Flemish painters lent their purple-draped Madonnas nursing baby Jesus. Nor was it the sweet smile of Kuan-Yin, goddess of fecundity and fertility, as we have often seen her painted on silk or sculpted in the ivory of distant China. No, this smile of Remedios's was too inhumanly languid to be comparable to those I have

101

mentioned. Springing from some unknown region of be-
ing, it had struck me in a region of the heart equally
unsuspected. Some of us have perhaps already seen this
sort of smile in a dream; its subtlety cannot survive one's
awakening. All that endures of it is a disturbance, incom-
municable and yet tenacious, that dissipates slowly like a
smell or a pain. Lastly, if you, reader, will permit me to
attribute the expression of a smile to a chaos of sterile
lava, I will say that this smile was the smile of Cecilia
itself.

The rest hardly deserves to be told. When the lights of
the cafe were turned off, Rosita and Juan were still at the
far end of the bar deep in their lovers' tête-à-tête, which
had been interrupted from time to time during the
evening only by the requirements of the customers in the
room.

"Adam," Remedios asked me in her somewhat harsh
voice, kissing me on the doorstep, "when are you going
to come to my house?"

As she moved away with Don Sebastian, I too disap-
peared among the sandy lanes in which my rope soles
made not a sound.

Sitting down with my back nicely wedged against my
lava rock, my legs stretched out in front of me, I took out
of the canvas shopping bag the apple that Rosita had
slipped into it, as she did every day, along with the sand-
wiches for my lunch. In front of the desalinization plant,

a few green shrubs and two or three rosebushes in flower formed the only, and minuscule, garden on Cecilia. On the grille surrounding it, a sign in black letters on white forbid access to it. In my mouth, the taste of the sour apple mingled with the dazzling whiteness and the rustling of the foam on the breakers. My fingers smelled of fish. Remedios said that I carried on me the smell of the death of the fish.

The fan consisted of a light armature of bright bamboo blades on which had been glued a thin sheet of white paper thinly glazed like certain kinds of paper from Japan. When the object was folded up, each of its sections looked like a closed book. Open, it bore in its center, as its only decoration, a white fish swimming, depicted by means of two equally white patches, one suggesting the back and the other the belly. Like the imperceptible scales on the silky wing of a butterfly, the pigments laid down on the paper by the brush did not catch the light in identical ways, so that depending on the incline of the hand holding the fan, only one of these patches at a time seemed to come alive, while the other remained confused with the neutral white of the background.

When I bring up a sea bream or a rock mullet at the end of my line and glimpse, from my lava platform, the gray shadow of a back or the white shadow of a belly glimmering through the blue water, less than three feet down under the frothy surface of a wave, I rediscover very exactly that alternation of shimmering and fading, of brilliance and matte that was produced, in my childish hand and in the light of those days, by the painted fish swimming up the white blades of the fan.

Certain evenings, when Don Miguel and Don Sebastian are chatting about general subjects, when Juan, standing at the end of the bar, is courting Rosita, when the noisy soldiers are making the wood of their tables ring with the dominoes, looking at Remedios sitting near me, I see her being traversed, like the white fan, by shadows and gleams of light which no one but I can see. Or will probably ever see.

"*Querido*," she asks me with a smile, "are you still thinking about your fish?"

"Remedios," I say, smiling back at her, "what do you know about my fish?"

Don Sebastian watches me genially. Genial Don Sebastian, you may be quite capable of caring for your indolent soldiers. You can't do anything for simple loneliness.

The moment has come, reader, to give you, among the many images reflected by other images, the place in my story which the painter used to reserve for the Donor, a grave and discreet personage who by his presence sealed the necessary alliance between his century and the dreams of the creator. That place of honor goes to you by right.

For isn't it in fact you, silent travelling companion, who

with your patient eyes illuminate my pages one by one? You who, like Ariadne rescuing Theseus, guide my steps through the living labyrinth I have built around me? You who, finally, by casting light at every moment upon my hesitant progress with the lamp of your experience, widen the field of my own horizon? For these reasons, and others you know better than I, it is only fair that you should appear in the very foreground of the picture.

Every saltwater fish, they say, has its corresponding freshwater fish. Thus, the marine half-sister of the melancholy carp would be the wrasse, with its vivid colors and large scales, whose rather stale-tasting flesh is appreciated by the islanders, who eat it fried, as carp is eaten in many areas. Fished by line in rocky water, the voracious wrasse requires a bait of crustacians or shellfish.

In this way, using sea snails pulled from their shells and strung on my hook as though on a brochette—a procedure that had left on my fingers, besides a tenacious smell of gunpowder, indelible dark purple stains—I had caught three good-sized wrasse, one yellow and two red.

I hadn't heard him come. But all of a sudden, I knew he was there behind me. Sitting on his heels, his eternal mocking smile on his lips, he was silently watching me. Naturally, he hadn't sounded the horn; he had slipped down like an Indian between the rocks, in the hope of discovering some secret or other to do with my fishing.

"Juan," I said, indicating by my glance the three wrasse

that were cleaned and lined up separate from the other fish on the stone, "see those three—do you want to know how I caught them? I caught them with sardines. With sardines—yes, really."

His smile was replaced by an expression of incredulous surprise.

"Sardines?" he couldn't help murmuring. "That's the first time anyone's ever caught a wrasse with a sardine!"

On the way back, Juan, who seemed perplexed, remained taciturn; the Land Rover seemed to me to lurch about less than usual on the stony track. When he applied the brakes behind the bakery, the sun was setting at the far end of the Rio. The boats of the squid fishermen were still out at sea. After I climbed down from the Land Rover, I took the three wrasse out of the metal pail where I had put my fish and gave them to him, for him to present to Rosita.

Three sorts of fish have gotten caught on my lines: the ones that, like the repulsive moray, allow themselves to be pulled up out of the water without offering more resistance than a heavy bundle of floating seaweed; those that fight the fisherman by zigzaging furiously back and forth parallel to the shore; and lastly, those that dive resolutely toward the bottom in the direction of the open sea. Each, in its own way, hopes to find salvation in flight.

Might I suspect that Juan, my indelicate driver, was most like the last sort of fish, the noblest of the three?

Less than two miles from my rock, Mount Claire rises up out of the ocean. The small island has the elongated form of a giant cetacian looming out of the water before it immediately plunges back in. Its half-submerged maw is an ancient crater, split down the middle, whose missing part, torn out long ago by a violent explosion from the volcano, has been swallowed up by the sea. The loud foam of the waves streams without respite down its brown and black flanks, striped in all directions by pink and violet scars. Mount Claire owes its name to this whiteness, as dazzling in broad daylight as bolts of forked lightning on a stormy night. Its cliffs, which fall sheer on all sides into the ocean, make the islet inaccessible, except to the sea birds that nest in the folds of its eviscerated hump.

As you sit facing that marine sphinx, tormented by cold waves, hold fast in your hands, Adam, the line that connects your life, beyond the restless surface of the waves, to another life not yet known to you. Hold the lifeline and don't go to sleep there in the sun: an unforeseeable surge could well carry you off, too.

Although the clock in the cafe never showed the exact hour—because the face no longer had its glass, the continuous stirring of the air by the vanes of the fan opposite it had to be slowing down the motion of the hands—it was after eleven in the evening when a clamor arose from the direction of the sea. The clouds that had gathered over the Rio were darkening the night. On the jetty, from the top of a mast, a powerful flare equipped with a reflector, such as those that light up stadiums at night, projected its glare over the sea straight up from the quay. In a semi-circle in the area thus illuminated, a dozen fishermen and as many excited young boys were pulling with all their strength on the two ends of a rope in order to haul up something heavy and invisible. A form rounded like a glass cloche soon emerged with a churning of the foam, brown and gleaming, a large, protuberant eye on either side of it. At this apparition, a fresh clamor of joy resounded under the projector and the haulers pressed on all the more energetically. A few minutes later, caught by the rope under its enormous fins which undulated down around it like a cape, the giant ray was dragged onto the sand where it struggled with pitiful, awkward convulsions, while its captors set to bludgeoning its cowled head. When the creature was dead, they abandoned its flaccid, shapeless cadaver at the edge of the beach. Then they scattered into the night. In the restored silence, the projector was doused on this grotesque end.

I saw Juan spit on the ground in disgust at the far end of the bar, where he had watched the scene through the window without moving.

"It isn't even edible," commented Don Sebastian at our table.

What motive might inspire a thoughtful, well-read man
to embark one summer evening on a large white boat and
travel miles and miles over the ocean in order to go fish-
ing with a rod and line on a desolate shore, all alone face
to face with the empty horizon? I can rule out entertain-
ment right away. Unless one wants to cure one ailment
with another, there is no boredom equal to that of the
long hours spent in the sun and wind, waiting uncom-
fortably for the random bite that will amuse one for a
moment. The attraction of silence, repose, and solitude,
you will say? Nothing is more fatiguing nor more deaf-
ening than the repeated din of the sea breaking the same
waves over the same rocks, not to speak of the blinding
reflection of the light on the water. What remains is the
opportunity to meditate away from domestic upheavals?
Take a look at the fishermen of this island, lined up every
evening at sunset on the treetrunk that lies along the base
of a wall and serves as a public bench in front of Don
Miguel's cafe. They sit side by side like penguins on an
icebank, staring straight ahead. Their empty eyes are the
pathetic reflection of the emptiness of their minds at the
end of a life devoted to fishing. Is that a fate to be envied?
No, believe me, all these pretexts are misleading. What
can induce a man to take ship one fine day for the pur-
pose of going fishing far away from home is completely
inexplicable. Unless that man doesn't really have a
"home." Unless that man, in flight and without a home
port, sets off one beautiful afternoon from Cadiz (pre-

cisely where Jonah, that other fugitive, thought he could take refuge from the commands of his God), and finds himself, after two days and two nights of voyaging, in some sense vomited up by the white vessel on the wild coast of Cecilia. And once he has landed in this place, impressed by the similarity between the dead landscape he sees before him and that other dead landscape he sees within him, he then thinks he has discovered, in the concealed mirror of what lives under the seas, something that might restore a spark of life in him. Or: crushed by the emptiness he feels under the sky, above his horizon, he wants to know if perhaps his sky is not under that horizon, transforming his supple fishing rod, for this purpose, into a lever capable of making the earth rock a few degrees.

One summer night, I happened to be on the deck of a boat anchored in the bottom of a cove; I had brought up a pail of sea water and sunk June's sponge into it, with the intention of sprinkling myself so as to cool off. At the bottom of the pail, the sponge became entirely phosphorescent and its form, shining like a star, seemed to rediscover, even unto its tiniest folds, a purely luminous and spectral life. When I sank my hand into the water to grasp it, my hand, too, began to shine, and from the sponge which I squeezed in my fingers, a sheaf of light blue sparks came out, surrounded by bubbles of light, as delicate and lively as those which Médé used to fan out of the coal fire at nightfall on the flags of the peristyle.

What relation, even deferred, can one establish between those two sources of sparks? Certainly none at all. But it does happen that after sunset one's mind is quick to form links, causelessly, among the phenomena that have impressed it.

Plato compared the Sophist to an angler. He even coined a word for his comparison: ἡ ἁλιευτικὴ, the alieutics, sister to maieutics.

In angling (here I am excluding, as Plato does, all other forms of fishing, such as fishing with a net, a pot, a spear, a bow, or a rifle), it is customary to distinguish, as in the ancient *iambe*, two consecutive times: a brief time followed by a long time. The *bite*, then the emergence of the fish from the water. These two times differ not only in duration, but in character, being essentially opposites. Without underestimating the importance of the second of these times (the one prefered by most fishermen) I myself favor the first.

The *bite* is the sign—in fact the only sign the fisherman receives since, unlike the hunter, he can't see his prey—of the presence of a fish at the end of his line. This sign of life that comes to him from the depths of the sea, however rapid it may be, contains in its principle the whole of fishing. For what follows—hooking the fish and then bringing it up (whatever may be the skill and experience required by these operations)—is only the accomplishment of this principle. At the moment of the tremor, the fisherman knows where he stands in the whole business: the fish; its size and weight; his chances of wresting it from the sea or losing it.

What gives the *bite* its singular character above all is that the fish is responsible for it while the only thing the fisherman can do, at the moment it occurs, is to remain alert, to keep watch blindly, but without impatience or annoyance, for the ineffable moment of the sign of recognition. When this comes in a lightning flash, all the time that preceded it and all the time that will come after it is in some way gathered up in the brief tremor. So that one can say that in the moment of the *bite* the fisherman holds in his hand, by grace of an invisible fish, his past and his future both.

Afterwards, the roles are reversed. In the struggle that follows the *bite*, the fisherman takes the initiative and tries to keep it. It's a much more down-to-earth business. A business concluded by death.

I won't dwell on what radically divides fishermen from sailors. I will only say this: they share the sea in the same way that the bear and the fox in the fable shared a field. The fishermen rule the upper part; the sailors the lower part. Their interests intersect. Without meeting, they go their own ways.

Now the line shivered; and as it shivered, it tightened from ring to ring along the flexible rod that arced under the weight. The fish, its head held high under the water as it fought with great thrashes of its tail, was slowly hauled up toward the light. Under the surface of the waves the patches of shadow and brightness began to alternate until, borne by a swell that supported its body one last time, it was deposited on a shelf at the foot of the rock. Seized by the gills, freed of the hook, it was thrown on the dry stone where, its maw gaping, its dorsal fin erect, it continued to arc in the empty air, its body shaken at intervals by spasms of suffocation. Except for the convulsive rustling of its scales on the lava, rather like the rustling of wings, there was no noise to signal its mute death-throes. When its gills had ceased to open in the air, when its strength no longer vibrated in the wind, the black stripes of its cloak very rapidly grew indistinct and turned pale. Whereas its eyes remained transparent, its entire body dimmed. They say a fish loses a portion of its weight in the moment that its life departs.

In my dream, the spire of the Chrysler Building was ablaze, every scale flaming, white in the sun like molten tin.

113

"I dreamed," Aerea said to me in my dream, "that the spire was burning, and the fire cast its livid gleams as far as the leaves of the tall trees in Central Park. And it was your fault, Adam! Your fault and no one else's!"

The fishermen who brought back his body had found it floating between two waters, at the entrance to the Rio not far from the spot where they usually dropped their nets. Rosita bent over the hand that stuck out from the canvas and took the chromium-plated watch off the wrist. At that moment, she lifted her arm to smoothe back a lock of hair that had escaped from her bun and was dangling down between her temple and her arched eyebrow. Her downy armpit suddenly reminded me of the single quick beat of the wings of a black butterfly lost in the midst of the light. Then I thought of the empty carapaces of the crabs in the rocks. And I moved away.

With a quick motion, Remedios tossed her half-consumed cigarette to the bottom of the steps, where it went out in the sand. Behind us, despite the late hour, the windows of the *Green House* were still lit. Except for the rumbling of the waves on the beach, the night was perfectly silent.

"The other girls have already left. It's just you and me alone here, now, Adam."

114

In the half-light, her voice was rougher and warmer than under the bare lighbulbs in Don Miguel's cafe.

I can't imagine, I thought suddenly, that the voice of Cranach the Younger's Eve could have been any different. And "Cranach the Elder" would be an ideal name for an extinct volcano.

Remedios was talking to me. I listened without interrupting. Leaning forward, as usual, her eyes gleaming under her long, pale eyelids, she was talking tranquilly about her life. Every time she bent forward to shake her cigarette ash off toward the bottom of the steps, the movement she made revealed the roundness of her little breasts under the overlapping panels of her blouse. Listening to her, I saw again the morning's procession, the boats on the Rio, the triangular flames of the colored flags snapping in the breeze, the flowers and pink and green paper garlands fastened along the masts and shrouds; I saw again the foamy wakes sparkling in the sun and I imagined Juan's mocking smile hovering over the nautical parade being offered him as a form of farewell. I wouldn't have been surprised to find him listening to the radio at the wheel of the Land Rover when I returned, to hear him say, when he saw me:

"Well, Adam, where shall I drive you today?"

But that morning, when I returned, the Land Rover was no longer behind the bakery.

I didn't bring back any fish from my last outing. I was fishing at night, in the spot Juan had driven me to most

often, in the northern part of Cecilia. The wind, after
blowing in squalls all day, had lost a little of its force and
the starry sky appeared among the clouds at irregular
intervals, revealing, when it did, the outline of Mount
Claire on the crests of the waves. The sea was high; the
swell, coming in before the wind from the open sea,
carved out enormous masses of water that broke on the
platform drowned in darkness. Then the din of the waves
and the foam, which fell down in an icy rain on my shoul-
ders, made the air and rock echo like a hollow theater
stage. Each breaker, as it withdrew, left behind it a phos-
phorescent train that in its turn descended the slope with
the noise of a cataract, redoubled by each new vertigi-
nous breath drawn by the ocean.

At two in the morning, the violence of the assaults
became so formidable that I had to give up fishing. Hold-
ing my equipment, I scaled the rocks and found refuge on
the highest steps of the foam-covered, resonant amphi-
theater of lava. Contemplating the chaos at my feet, I
waited for daybreak.

Under the first rays of sun, even though the sea had
gone back down, the tempest was still raging. The wind
scored the surface of the water with short white crests.
The flanks of the dunes behind me were tinged with pink
lights. But the cones of the volcanoes remained gray, in-
sensitive to the morning light.

The volcanoes are not just one more element in the
scorched landscape of Cecilia. They are the very sub-
stance of the island. They are this dead island of which
each parcel of rock, baked in the inner ovens of the planet,
is forever resistant to anything that might come from out-
side to soften its savagery. The two main volcanoes of

Cecilia, which has about a dozen, have been christened Big Tit and Little Tit. But only burning lava has risen as nourishing milk in these now sterile craters, joining fast, in eruption after eruption, the great mummifed body of the island to its sarcophagous.

No fragrant meadow will ever undulate over its wrinkled slopes: one might as soon hope to see grass grow in a pot that contains no earth. It is a chaos open to the sky, without protective covering. The fires of the sun, which can bleach stone formed at the bottom of the sea, has no effect on the black rock that obeys only its own laws, attentive, perhaps, like a fisherman on his rock, to the least sign betraying an underlying life.

At eleven in the morning, my back turned to the wind and the sea, I at last saw the volcanoes gradually change color. At the hour when the oblique rays of the sun begin to crush shapes and colors under an excess of luminosity, I saw the gloomy volcanoes slowly turn various shades of brown and violet, light and dark gray, ocher and pink, bringing into play all the nuances and intensities of its own particular rainbow. I had the impression that they were fabricating before my eyes their own light and their own colors, in the same way that certain people secrete, at times, an unhabitual beauty whose ephemeral depositaries they are, as though nature were lending them this very disturbing increase in charm that indifferently diffuses around it consolation or desolation.

When the sun began to go down in the sky, again coloring the surfaces of things, the volcanoes returned to their inert gray. At that point I started back to the pueblo.

"Visit me, Adam," Aerea said to me in her melodious voice, at the other end of the wire, beyond the ocean.

Is it dawn? A name emerges on the uniform surface of the water. The sea appears to be covered in a film of pale gold that undulates endlessly its nacreous reflections. A name tears apart the delicate layer of gold. Or is it the back of a playful porpoise? The name dissolves in the water. It isn't yet dawn. It's the middle of the night; the time for remembering. Don't fall asleep, Adam! In the heart of this yellow fog wrapping around you, you perceive a bottomless fault. Remember! Other nacreous letters form other names that intertwine and give birth to new names. Our bodies, well harmonized in love, were translucent under the Manhattan light. Who can shake off the burden of his name? Dreams roll their soft undulations over our memories, which we retrieve undamaged, so to speak, when we awaken. In November, the trees lose their leaves; the winter tides unload the dead wood from the ocean, covering the beaches with it; relieved of the weight of the snow, pine trees lift their heads in April and in the beds of dry mountain streams the pink laurel flowers in summer. But nothing lightens the yoke, heavier from year to year, of the name that we bear. Yes, that we bear, throughout our lives, in the deepest part of us like an insoluble calculation. Of course, it would have been better not to begin! But the idea of a beginning haloed in easy promises is indissociably linked to that bad calculation. It is the spike that sways under our cranium, that we run away from. When God called Adam, at first Adam turned a deaf ear. Hearing himself named for the second time, he presented himself before The One who had called him; and he pleaded guilty. Ever since that case, where a good lawyer was definitely lacking, we have been in a fine mess, all of us! Even if we were to attach end to end those winding-sheets embroidered with our initials, we wouldn't manage to escape from the old genealogical tree whose dead leaves never fall, thrusting indefinitely up to the sky new leaves soughing in the azure like the scales of a rattlesnake. This, all the insomniacs in the world will tell you.

And since everything on this earth must have a beginning, here is what the beginning of this book was: our bodies intertwined on the sheet in the Manhattan bedroom, Aerea, on top of me, let fall on my lips, as she came, these words in which honey was tenderly mingled with venom:

"Don't forget me! Don't forget me!"